THE ELLE DECOR HOME

THE ELLE DECOR HOME

filipacchi
publishing

CONTENTS

LIVING ROOMS

THE LIVING ROOM IS PERHAPS THE ONE ROOM THAT IS MOST CENTRAL TO THE "HOME." BECAUSE IT IS THE ROOM WE LIVE IN AND THE PLACE WHERE WE ENTERTAIN, TODAY'S LIVING ROOM MUST BE BOTH CONVIVIAL AND COMFORTABLE. WE HAVE COME A LONG WAY FROM THE POMP AND CEREMONY OF THE RECEPTION ROOM OF THE EARLY 20TH CENTURY. INDEED, IN THE MODERN ERA, LIVING ROOMS HAVE BECOME KNOWN AS PLACES THAT ARE GOOD TO LIVE IN, AND WHERE EVERYONE LIKES TO LINGER. THEY OFFER A CHANCE TO EXPRESS REFINEMENT AND TO SHOW OFF DIFFERENT DECORATIVE STYLES, USING EVERY POSSIBLE OPPORTUNITY TO COME UP WITH MYRIAD COMBINATIONS THAT CAN BE CREATED BY COMBINING SOFAS AND SETTEES, ARMCHAIRS AND COFFEE TABLES, ORGANIZED AROUND A BOOKCASE OR ARRANGED BESIDE A FIREPLACE. SOME DESIGNERS DARE TO INTRODUCE ECCENTRICITY INTO THESE LIVING SPACES, HAPPILY MIXING DIFFERENT STYLES AND HUES. OTHERS STRESS SIMPLICITY AND SOFTNESS BY CREATING SUMPTUOUS WHITE LIVING ROOMS.

SOFA
NOOKS

THESE ARE PLACES CONDUCIVE TO CHATTING AND RELAXING WITH FRIENDS. CORNER SETTEES, BANQUETTE SEATS, CLUB CHAIRS AND CHAISES LONGUES, EMBELLISHED WITH CUSHIONS AND PLAIDS. SOFA NOOKS OPT FOR COMFORT AND WARMTH IN A MOST ELEGANT WAY.

Above. Anthony Collett chose a bold, neo-Baroque style to enliven the living room of an old London house. A burst of powerful colors gives this room its vibrant, cheerful feel. The walls are covered with gold leaf, and the two wing chairs are upholstered in military baize, with shawls and cushions designed by G. Flower. The curtains are in red and purple velvet, while the under curtains are in bright yellow cotton.

Left. The bold-striped sofa was designed by Collett himself. The cushions are by Julia Pinès. To the right of the sofa, an early 20th-century ecclesiastical table.

Above. In his Paris home, young antiques dealer Alexandre Biaggi shows his flare for combining objects in a most unexpected way. In the living room, the atmosphere harkens back to the 1950s and '60s. Two Serge Mouille lights have been hung from the ceiling. The matching, zebra-striped cushions and two candlesticks complete this play of symmetry. Set no less shrewdly on the coffee table are ashtrays from the Capron studio, which call to mind the ceramics of Vallauris.

Right. East meets West, in style, here at this Istanbul residence where Anouska Hempel has juggled with harmonies in ginger, black and stone. This area of the living room also doubles as a screening room. The screen is cleverly concealed beneath the ceiling, above the windows. The sofas in thick, dark-colored Indian cotton, are partly covered with cashmere rugs. On the low chest tables, a black lacquer tray, circa 1930, plays host to two silver salvers holding Moroccan matchboxes.

SOFA NOOKS

Interior decorator Julie Prisca
has set the living room of
her Normandy home in sunny
colors. The furniture, which
she designed, fits perfectly
with the saffron-yellow walls
and the beams painted a
delicate, lagoon green. The sofa
is covered in bright, red cloth.
And on the covered armchairs,
a wool and angora buttoned
plaid. The top of the coffee
table is in oak that was gouged
out to create this handsome
motif. At the back of the room
stands an impressive piece of
regional furniture made of
fruitwood. Seagrass carpeting
covers the floor and provides
the perfect finishing touch to a
room that evokes the colors and
textures of a sunny marshland.

Above. Decorators David Champion and Anthony Collett have reorganized the space of this large London apartment, and designed much of the furniture in it, to boot. The 17th-century fireplace is set off by a very 20th-century photo of Pablo Picasso, which was taken by Irving Penn. Picasso's fixed gaze cuts through the creamy white hues of the living room. On either side of the fireplace, there are Collett- and Champion-designed loudspeakers doubling as stands for ancient Greek vases. The yellow- and grey-striped silk fabric of the chaise longue—designed by Christopher Gibbs—picks up the stripes of the curtains. The sofa, tables and lamps were also designed by Collett and Champion.

Right. In a village house on the Ile de Ré, on France's Atlantic coast, an L-shaped sofa surrounds a coffee table formed by two Bertoïa benches set side by side. The lamps are by David Hicks. On the windows, venetian blinds with thin wooden slats filter the light. At the far end of the living room, there is an elegant spiral staircase imported from London.

Left. Henri Becq, designer and founder of the Modénature furniture store in Paris, lives in an apartment featuring a condensed version of the style that has earned him such success—a simple, sober place that is easy to live in. In the living room, two chaises longues in string linen act as sofas. Cotton cloth curtains by Chantal Benoist were chosen to dress up the windows. They can be drawn from wall to wall along the fixed traverse rod. The standard lamps were designed by Karl Kroener for Modénature. On the wall, collages by Ariane Lassaigne.

Above. Monic Fisher, founder of the Blanc d'Ivoire company, has chosen a timeless, easy-to-live-in style for her Saint-Germain-des-Prés home. The two large sofas in the main living room are covered in linen. On the Le Corbusier leather sofa, a sand-colored quilt by Blanc d'Ivoire. On the coffee table by Gae Aulenti, bronze Japanese vases and silver-plated bowls make up the tablescape. Against the far wall, between the two French windows, there is a Kamakura sculpture by Georges Jeanclos.

Above. This duplex, with its double exposure, ivory walls and bleached parquet floors, is an open invitation to light. It was decorated by Monic Fisher. The immaculate sofa is upholstered with linen. The desk, made of granite and wrought iron, contrasts nicely with the furniture, which was all designed by Frédéric Méchiche. The stout, pale oak coffee table

has been hollowed out to conceal a spot. On the wall, a photo of Dora Maar.

Above. This house in Paris gives off a country ambience. It features coir matting on the floor and gray lacquered beams. The sofas are covered with canvas sheet. A Louis XVI commode and a roll-top desk are visible in the back. The painting is from Galerie La Scala.

Above. This private, 19th-century mansion was decorated by Hubert Le Gall. The living room was divided so as to create two independent areas made one by the style. Above the sofa, a work by Tamara de Lempicka is flanked by bronze cogwheels by Le Gall. In the foreground, the main part of the living room has been furnished with 1940s-style armchairs and lamps.

Right. The owner of this apartment in Lyon entrusted architect Rémi Tessier with the task of decorating. The leather and woven linen sofa was made by Tessier. Above it, two pictures are set on a small shelf designed specifically for them. To the right, on the stone table, a lamp made of wenge wood with a silk shade.

AROUND
COFFEE TABLES

AT THE CENTER OF THE LIVING ROOM, FOR ALL TO LOOK AT, THE COFFEE TABLE IS OFTEN USED FOR DISPLAYING FLOWERS, BOOKS AND MUCH LOVED OBJECTS. THERE IS NO LACK OF IMAGINATION WHEN IT COMES TO MAKING USE OF MATERIALS. INTERIOR DECORATORS HAVE A FIELD DAY WITH: BAMBOO, BRONZE, GLASS, OAK AND SYCAMORE.

Left. In Manuel Canovas' living room, a rather whimsical coffee table made of bronze and glass, created by Diego Giacometti. The subtle, yet bright colors of the moquette show off this table to great advantage.

Above. A metal bed from India serves as a coffee table in Agnès Comar's home in Provence. On either side of the sofa, tables covered with long tablecloths are adorned with matching wooden lights, which Comar designed.

AROUND
COFFEE TABLES

A mixture of styles and an
intermingling of periods is
evident in Axel Vervoordt's
castle near Antwerp. On the
flattened bamboo coffee table,
designed by the antiques
dealer-*cum*-interior designer,
there are symbolic ivory objects
from the Ming period,
a rectangular ceramic tray
from the Han period,
and a precious brown-glaze
vase with a bird's head spout
dating to the Khmer period.
The armchair from the
Louis XIII period is covered
with antique wool fabric.
On the table and in the
18th-century pine cupboard
from the Rhineland, a
collection of Sukhothaï pottery.

Left. This table, designed by Olivier Gagnère for Artelano, is distinctive for its simplicity. The bleached oak blends with the colors of the 1930s carpet and those of the screen. Both were flea market finds.

Above. In this collector's living room, a decorative style made up of a thousand and one precious objects. In the middle, the coffee table by Emile-Jacques Ruhlmann consists of two tabletops, one above the other. The armchairs around it are by the same designer. The display cabinet is by Prinz, and the table lamp and floor lamp are by Tiffany. The glassware collection is by Daum, and the glasses are from Venice.

Left. In the Provençal home of a collector, we find this generously proportioned Anglo-Indian coffee table. Much of it is covered with fine books, which seems in keeping with the numerous works of art lining the walls. The 18th-century Provençal armchairs, together with the sofa, the carpet and the lampshades, all in warm colors, form a harmonious whole.

Above, right. For these coffee tables, Yves Taralon has used two old X-shaped stands, on which he has laid birchwood tops. The 17th-century stone fireplace is flanked by vases from Anduze.

Below, right. On the oak parquet floor, a practical table made for friendly gatherings. The walls are painted yellow and ochre, and the sofa is lit by two wrought iron floor lamps.

29

AROUND
COFFEE TABLES

In the living room of this
early 20th-century castle in
Flanders, the oak floor is made
of freight train planks. On it,
Lionel Jadot has arranged
a Louis XVI daybed and a
carpet made from a Berber tent.
This young interior designer
has chosen subtle shades of
color—such as pale gray and
beige—which highlight the
eclectic collection of objects
and furniture. Jadot designed
all the seating, which was
subsequently made in the
Vanhamme family business.

Above. In this living room, nestled beneath a mezzanine, interior designer Rémi Tessier has created a play of right angles and straight lines. The table is made of dark sycamore and was designed by Patricia and Philippe Hurel. It stands out because of its elegant simplicity, and sits gracefully on a plum-colored rug. Philippe Hurel also designed the chaise longue. The chairs are covered in a tawny leather, and the low, armless easy chair is covered in tobacco-colored wild silk. In the back, to the right, an oil painting by Pincemin. The lamp to the left was created by Tessier for Jean-Michel Delisle.

Above. In Ixelles—the comfortable, residential area of Brussels—we find a living room full of light and sharp contrasts. The design of the room relies on faultless finishing touches orchestrated by interior designer Axel Verhoustraeten to achieve a decidedly contemporary effect. The wooden coffee table is a Christian Liaigre creation, as is the jute fabric covering the sofa. The floor lamp was designed by Verhoustraeten. On the wall, a series of desert photos by Sylvie Durimier. Easy living is the prevailing theme in this living room that places great emphasis on wood and white.

AROUND
COFFEE TABLES

In this living room, featuring
superb 17th-century oak
woodwork, a coffee table with
a Gilbert Poillerat travertine top
is supported by globes. It stands
on a carpet created by Arbus.
To the left, the oak stools and
bronze and leather armchair
are also Arbus creations.
Behind the sofa, Poillerat
wall lights illuminate a picture
of a Japanese notable.
The matching armchairs are by
Arbus, and the furniture comes
from the Yves Gastou gallery.

AROUND COFFEE TABLES

Catherine Memmi has opted
for three main colors for her
Haussmann-like apartment in
Saint-Germain-des-Prés: matte
white, sandy and black. The
colors go well together and lend
this brightly lit living room a
simple and assertive elegance.
The long sofa is covered in
white cotton cloth. The floor
is covered with a large, black
sisal carpet. The wenge table is
a Catherine Memmi creation.
On it, we see a square ceramic
dish with Moka candles and
photo albums in black nubuck.
On the wall, a painting by
Hilton McConnico.

Above. Yves Gastou and Jean Galvani are responsible for the look of this large Toulouse apartment. Gastou brought together a collection of neoclassical pieces from the 1940s, and Galvani introduced a touch of spare design to the premises. The living room is dominated by the impressive Arbus bookcase made in the 1950s. The marble coffee table was designed by Gae Aulenti. The furniture is made of oak. A pair of Venetian glass lamps from the 1940s stand on the tables beside the sofa.

Above. A play of symmetries prevails in this living room in a triplex converted by architect Rémi Tessier. The central axis is formed by the two bamboo coffee tables. The furniture is decked out in both muted and dazzling colors, which contrast with the beige hue of the walls painted in marble powder. The sofas, in leather and woven linen, and offset by embroidered cushions, were designed by Tessier, as was the red bench. On either side of the window with its linen curtains, a pair of black oak bookshelves that were also designed by Tessier.

AROUND THE
FIREPLACE

ALL IT TAKES IS THE MAGIC OF A WOOD FIRE, AND SUDDENLY A CITY APARTMENT CAN BE TRANSFORMED INTO A COUNTRY HOME. WHETHER THEY ARE MADE OF MAHOGANY OR MARBLE, STONE OR PINE, FIREPLACES ADD A FRIENDLY, WELCOMING TOUCH TO LIVING ROOM DECORATION.

Left. Above this 19th-century marble fireplace, against a stone background painted in trompe-l'œil by Alain Ozanne, Jacques Leguennec has arranged various objects: a 17th-century wooden mannequin, a chimaera, marble and alabaster ruins, and Pascale Laurent watercolors.

Above. This stone fireplace, designed by Guy Bontemps in the 1930s style, is framed from floor to ceiling by two long light strips in black ironwork. The color scheme for the living room was inspired by the 1930s vases created by David.

Left. Maïmé Arnodin's fireplace, made up of mirror shards, was designed by César. The sculpture, entitled "La Poulette," is also a César work. The small chain curtains acting as a fire guard were commissioned from San Diego.

Right. In the home of Patrick and Yveline Frèche, the raised fireplace is made of painted brick. A broad surround offers plenty of room on either side of the hearth for sculptures and photos. The coffee table is made of painted ash.

AROUND THE FIREPLACE

Above. In the home of architects Jean-Louis and Mado Mellerio, this very distinctive shade and uneven effect for the fireplace was achieved by mixing concrete with clay. On either side of the fireplace stand a sofa and an armchair designed by Jean-Louis and Mado. Both are covered with a brightly colored fabric by Zoltan. The Ettore Sottsass sculpture comes from the Yves Gastou gallery.

Right. In front of Kenzo's Japanese bedroom, the fireplace is encircled by a metal, mesh fire guard. It stands center stage, asserting itself as the main feature of the decor. To the left, a traditional Japanese lantern.

Left. Joëlle Mortier Vallat wanted to transform her extremely classical, white marble, 19th-century fireplace, so she painted it in leopard spot trompe-l'œil. A jumble of wonderful things are on display here—including an architect's light from 1910, a bullfighting lithograph by Picasso, a pair of American arts and crafts-style candlesticks, and a 19th-century bronze Japanese vase.

Right. An ingenious idea to revamp and rejuvenate a classical fireplace: Paint it white. Here, a perfect opportunity to display a collection of Staffordshire pottery.

Left. The home of couturier Joseph features the elegance and simplicity of a marble fireplace. A triple recess merges it with the wall—a modern and original design.

Above. In the home of interior designer Daniel Kiener, the fireplace set into the wall seems to be a natural extension of the bookshelves. In the foreground, English armchairs from India.

Above. A fireplace with character fits in perfectly with the pale wood of the parquet floor, the furniture and the trompe-l'œil woodwork by Nathalie Mahiu. French actor Pierre Arditi crowned this warm decor with sofas designed by Yves Halard and pale curtains that give an added brightness to the living room. The pine desk dates from the 17th century. The antique kilims are flea market finds, and the armchairs are Anne Gayet creations.

Above. Warm hues and candles create an intimate ambience in the home of Yves and Michelle Halard. The decoration of this living room is all about things natural and authentic. It features broad planked, rough pine parquet, the branch of a tree, and a basket overflowing with balls of moss. The armchairs are covered with a fabric that goes well with the quilt of toile de Jouy hanging on the wall. The low table was designed by Yves Halard.

AROUND THE FIREPLACE

Rustic comfort and a spirit
of Scandinavia prevail at
Michèle Rédélé's home in
Megève, in the French Alps.
The 18th-century timberwork
has been dismantled, plank
by plank, and reassembled
in exactly the same manner.
The coffee table, designed by
Rédélé was made by Alain
Grosset, a Megève blacksmith.
The sofas are covered with a
woolen cloth from Bonneval.
The Manufactor lights add
a contemporary touch.

BOOK NOOKS

PARDON THE PUN, BUT BOOKCASES SPEAK VOLUMES ABOUT THE
TASTES OF THOSE DISPLAYING BOOKS AND ART ON THEIR SHELVES.
THESE PIECES OF FURNITURE NOT ONLY INCREASE AVAILABLE STORAGE
SPACE, BUT ALSO SERVE AS FULLY FLEDGED FEATURES OF THE DECOR.

Left. Designer Henri Becq designed these three bookcases, reaching from floor to ceiling. He deliberately set them slightly apart, so as to give space to the shelving. The bookcases are made of rosewood-hued poplar. Around the varnished ash table, three Directoire chairs covered in string linen. The floor lamp is a Modénature creation, and the two small lamps were designed by Julie Prisca.
Above. In this Left Bank apartment, the oak and mesh bookcases are divided by stucco columns. The armchair, reupholstered in a striped velvet, is a Boussac creation, and the candelabra-type lamp is the work of Annick Clavier.

The art of living is perfected
in this Greenwich Village
living room. The owner of
this apartment has cleverly
created maximum space from
a minimum of volume.
The rendering that once
covered the walls has been
removed and replaced by
painted wooden planks to make
the room look larger. On the
far wall, picture shelves display
works by Geoffrey Holder and
Le Groumellec. The shelves are
adjacent to a narrow bookcase
that allows the volumes to
remain upright. The television
is set into the wall. On the
coffee table, a collection of
silver candlesticks and an
articulated lamp from Camoin.
The color white is everywhere
and is enhanced by the bright
colors of the pictures.

Above. The harmonious
balance in this Saint-Germain-
des-Prés duplex is the result
of a design by Laurent Bourgois
that was based on a 19th-
century studio work.
The architect-*cum*-interior
designer has emphasized light
and juggled with the mansarded
volumes. The extensive
bookshelves—which fit perfectly
in this living room—were made
by Mac Déco. Behind the
Hugues Chevalier sofa, covered
with a Pierre Frey flannel
fabric, stands a Marina Donati
bronze. Books fill the shelves,
and curios and sculptures are
spread out over the coffee table
by Bertoia. But the room retains
a serene atmosphere because it

has been so perfectly organized. **Above.** This Saint-Germain apartment is quite different. It is made up of things the owners couldn't resist and is furnished exclusively with tactile materials, wood, marble and whitewash. In its sumptuous volumes, the room manages to display an austere beauty. The bookcases have been painted with the same coating as the walls. Above them, trompe-l'œil paintings of books, vases and baskets have been added to restore the proportions—which were not always quite right. The "Champagne Cork" chairs come from the Cour Intérieure gallery.

Above. In Frédéric Méchiche's Marais home, the decor was inspired by the 18th and 19th centuries. The walls of the library are covered with 18th-century woodwork.

In front of the window, the interior designer has put a Napoleon III sofa covered with mauve satin. The old parquet is made of rough oak planks that were found at a

salvage yard. A Moroccan table stands on a small North African rug, the stripes of which echo those of the chairs and chaise longue. The other chairs are covered with canvas sheet.

Above. In Jacques Leguennec's living room in Paris, near Saint-Germain-des-Prés, the books are arranged by theme in a set of limed oak bookcases that he designed, and that cover almost all of the walls. The two sofas facing each other are covered with canvas sheet. In the middle, two coffee tables bring out the symmetrical effects. In front of the window, a limed oak lectern, also designed by Jacques. The turned wooden lamp has been painted by Alain Ozanne.

BEDROOMS

WE LEAVE IT IN THE MORNING, NOSTALGICALLY. AND RETURN TO IT AT NIGHT, HAPPILY. WE SPEND ALMOST HALF OUR LIVES IN IT. SO IT IS ABSOLUTELY FUNDAMENTAL TO FEEL GOOD IN IT. THE BEDROOM IS THE MOST PRIVATE ROOM IN THE HOUSE—THE PLACE THAT SPEAKS VOLUMES ABOUT OUR TASTES AND OUR PERSONALITIES. WHEN IT COMES TO DECORATING THE BEDROOM, WE GIVE FREE REIN TO OUR DESIRES AND IMAGINATIONS, TRY TO STAMP OUR BEDROOM WITH THE HALLMARKS OF OUR LIVES. BUT THE BEDROOM IS ALSO A SHRINE TO IDLENESS. NOTHING IS SPARED WHEN IT COMES TO CREATE COMFORTS. THE BED IS THE KEY ELEMENT OF A BEDROOM'S DECORATION. WHEN SIZE PERMITS, BEDROOMS CAN BE TURNED INTO LIVING ROOMS, NO LESS. SOME PEOPLE EVEN SET UP THEIR OFFICE IN THEM, OR CREATE A SPACE FOR A SMALL LIBRARY. OTHERS MAKE ROOM FOR BATHTUB AND SINK.

BEDROOMS
FOR LIVING IN

BEDROOMS FOR LIVING IN ARE MUCH MORE THAN ORDINARY BEDROOMS. SURROUNDING THE BED MAY BE A LIBRARY OR AN OFFICE. BEDROOMS ARE THUS TRANSFORMED INTO ROOMS THAT ARE NICE TO LIVE IN EVERY MOMENT OF THE DAY.

Left. In this erstwhile studio in the heart of Paris, antique dealer Christian Sapet has created an intimate and eclectic setting, with books here, there and everywhere. The library consists of evenly spaced rough planks filling the wall from floor to ceiling.
Above. To make the bedroom appear bigger, Sapet installed two sliding mirrors, which cunningly lengthen the bookshelves and hide a dressing room beyond.

Above. The bedroom in this London apartment —which was revamped by interior designers David Champion and Anthony Collett, who also designed much of the furniture—displays a strong personality. The cushions match the 17th century carpet and pick out the blue of the Chinese vases placed atop a wardrobe designed to hide hi-fi equipment. The curtains are of silk taffeta, and the cream hues are well matched to the soft range of blues.

Above. For this New Jersey collector with a passion for windvanes and weathercocks, decorator Brigitte Semtob created a space where the emphasis is on airiness and the outdoors. This is a bedroom with clean lines, where the harmony comes mainly from the choice of delicate, complementary colors. The glass roof, like the side windows, makes the room very light. The furniture is of Canadian beech. Above the bed rests a statue of a horse, and to its left a 19th century copper centaur.

BEDROOMS
FOR LIVING IN

For the owners of this
apartment in the Left Bank
of Paris, decorator
Brigitte Semtob has chosen
sober colors so as to highlight
their art collection.
In the bedroom, the sheets
trimmed with red braid and
the cashmere bedspread add
a bright, dynamic touch,
breaking away from the
overall bluish feel. The relief
on board hung over the bed,
as well as the "Red Circle"
rug, are by Jean Arp.

Above. This bedroom reflects the white magic of a duplex completely converted by Frédéric Méchiche, who also designed the furniture. The decoration is based on an outward simplicity: ivory-colored walls, bleached oak parquet flooring, armchairs swathed in white linen and cream canvas slipcovers on either side of French windows leading to a terrace that runs the length of the apartment. To add contrast, Méchiche implemented a halogen light and a granite and wrought iron table. All these features combine to create a calming, sophisticated setting.

Above. In this village house in the Ile de Ré, on France's Atlantic coast, a large bedroom with bathroom incorporated combines originality with ingeniousness. The pine-paneled walls have been impregnated with bondex, a kind of milk paint that stops the wood from darkening. In the alcove, the sink and bathtub have been set in the same wood so they blend in with the rest of the room. On the floor, made of rubbed terra cotta slabs, an English pine table is flanked by a pair of chairs covered in white piqué.

Above. Decorator Michelle Halard, who designed this bedroom for her friends Jean-André and Geneviève Charrial, went after simplicity at all costs —be it in the colors or the floor coverings. As a result, the neutral tones accentuate the brightness and beauty of the raspberry-hued curtains, sheets and painted wooden shelves which are fitted to masonry uprights. The zinc lamp and the rug were designed by Yves Halard.

Above. This apartment in New York's Greenwich Village shows the practical spirit of a small bedroom organized around the bed, making it possible to get the most out of the available space. The charm of the open brickwork of the fireplace, together with the gold-colored woodwork is emphasized by the window, which floods the room with light. On either side of the fireplace, storage units combine bookshelves with drawer space. The bed stands on a North Carolina pine floor. A potentially cramped room that has been most cunningly done up.

In decorating the Provençal
farmhouse of her friend Sarah
Saint-George, Maxime de la
Falaise has mixed styles and
colors together with great
panache. The "portraits
bedroom," shows the daring
of a reined-in free spirit,
improvising around Polish and
Oriental themes. There is a lot
of imagination and originality
in the combination of different
prints—particularly for the
canopied bed, embellished with
embroidered fabrics and exotic
silks. But the most striking
feature is the use made of color.
Maxime has painted the walls
with colored distempers in
ocher and pistachio. The paint
was applied first with a brush,
then spread with a cloth.
Beyond the Moroccan rug,
two portraits of Maxime by
her father, Sir Oswald Birley,
frame the fireplace.

Above. This Provençal farmhouse, decorated by Jacques Grange for his friends Terry and Jean de Gunzburg, displays a wealth of details and patterns in a vast bedroom. Here we can clearly see the structure of the "bedroom-study-loggia-winter living room" for which he drew up the plans. Framing the bed are lamps and bedside tables by Vincent Corbière. On the right, there is a drawing by Wendy Artin and a 19th century Basque gourd. At the foot of the bed, which was designed by Vincent Corbière, is a sculpture by a young Spanish artist, "Yaguès," set on an Ethiopian mat. Precious decorative objects hailing from all over the world abound in this room, which places great emphasis on straight lines and right angles.

Above. Here we see the bedroom from another angle, showing the living room area. The sculpture wall made of "cocciopesto"—a mixture of egg shells and terra cotta—was designed by Jacques Grange for the Galerie Farnese. The oak and leather furniture is by Royère, and the pair of iron and leather armchairs were created by Giacometti for Jean-Michel Frank. The rug is by Georges Braque. On the upper, separating wall, reside frieze-like photos of Marilyn Monroe by Bert Stern.

Above. A harmony of camel-colored hues for this bedroom, with furniture designed by Frédéric Méchiche. The purity of the lines used in this resolutely contemporary style go perfectly with the comfort and warmth of the cashmere and the checkerboard oak paneling. The result is a luminous atmosphere that enhances the art collected by the owners—like this Keith Haring triptych, with its crisp graphic effects. The bedside lamps are by Ingo Maurer.

Above. With this bedroom, East meets West on the shores of the Bosphorus. Mehmet Bay and Zeynep Garan went to Anouska Hempel for their Istanbul home, and she designed its volumes. The decorator opted for a play of black and ginger hues, and this combination permits pleasant contrasts with the white and rust-colored stripes. The lacquered 16th century furniture and the windows, with their Japanese blinds, are all Oriental in inspiration. Acting as headboards, old cherrywood and ebony doors are set against walls covered with tadlakt. On the window sill, a majestic ebony lamp and porphyry bowls.

Left and above. Bill Blass was known to have asserted that color "distracts," which is why he used it with caution. Here, in his second home in New England, Blass played with somber, sober shades. The couturier's huge bedroom was a meeting room when this house was used previously as a tavern. The bed is covered in a patchwork quilt typical of New England. The staircase is not, as you might first think, a masterly work, but a surrealist sculpture. It is the only sign of fantasy amid a minimalist decoration that created a feeling of austere comfort. There are no curtains on the windows, but rather interior shutters.

ATTIC
BEDROOMS

SIMPLE PLEASURE: SLEEPING RIGHT UNDER THE ROOF... BY PLACING GREAT IMPORTANCE ON NATURAL MATERIALS, ATTIC BEDROOMS GO FOR AUTHENTICITY. THE BEAMS AND OPEN STONEWORK WHICH THEY PROUDLY DISPLAY LEND THEM A WARM, RUSTIC CHARM.

Left. This bedroom, in designer Julie Prisca's Normandy home, displays simplicity full of charm. The mix of painted woodwork, the quilted bedspread and tulle creates a very gentle atmosphere. **Above.** A Baroque touch for this Provence bedroom designed with African hues by Maxime de la Falaise for her friend Sarah Saint-George.

Left. In her manor house in the middle of the English countryside, Lady Weinberg has installed this bed—which she has designed like a bunk in a boat—in the garret. On the wall, broad bands of whitewash match the parquet flooring. On the left, a 19th century farmhouse chair in bleached oak.

Right. At Porquerolles, off France's Mediterranean coast, this bedroom in the attic reflects a tranquil modernity with its intentionally spare decoration. Its contrasting shades of color and the presence throughout of wood—here worked by Daniel and Olivier Pelenc—add a warm touch. The wall lights, seed merchant's furniture and armchairs call a certain colonial style to mind.

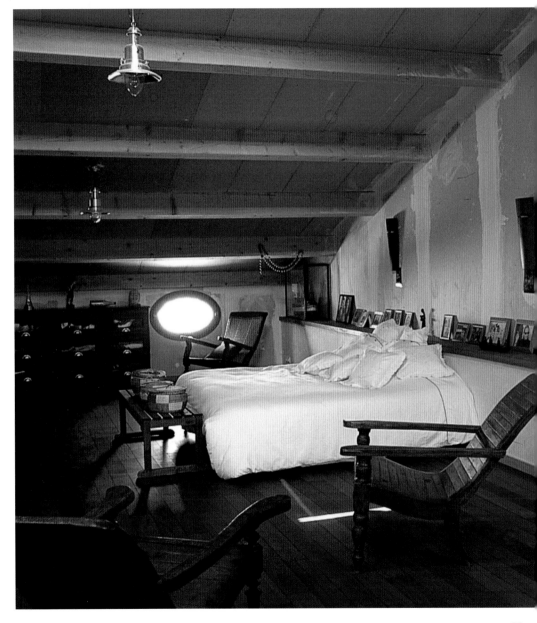

ATTIC BEDROOMS

Comfort and romanticism are
on exhibit in François d'Armor's
bedroom in the Bagnols Castle
hotel, located in the Beaujolais
region of France. Beneath the
original timberwork and beams,
the four-poster beds have been
trimmed with old toile de Jouy.
The club chairs have been
covered with linen slipcovers.
An authenticity created by
using of darkish wood,
lends a rustic allure to
this huge bedroom.

Left. The interior of this farmhouse—which rests at the foot of the Luberon range in southern France—combines Indonesian furniture and warm hues to create a decoration akin to the colonial style. The owners, Michèle and Paul Belaiche, were keen to have a bedroom that is perfect for living in. The floor, made of terra cotta tiles, is covered with rattan mats from Borneo. The low, bamboo table is from Java. The settee, buried beneath patterned cushions, comes from Indonesia. The leather armchairs are from the 1930s.

Right. This home of a Belgian collector illustrates a successful mix of genres expressing ethnic influences. A boxed-in area serves as both a headboard and a shelf for a collection of traditional objects, photos and a Russian Cubist painting. At the foot of the bed, art books are laid out on an Indonesian table. In the foreground, on the left, a Dogon ladder frames the room.

Left. This Harbour Island house in the Bahamas belongs to a person with a passion for architecture and decoration. This house, like a boat, was built entirely of timber. For the bedroom, the bed, which is based on an Indian model, was built on the spot. The patchwork bedspread and the collection of round boxes lend it a slightly "cottage-y" feel.

Right. A warm atmosphere abounds in the Boutchoux de Chavannes bedroom in the Bagnols Castle outbuildings. The room adopts a "country" style, at once simple and refined: The red-checked fabric surrounding the four-poster bed goes wonderfully well with the beams and open stonework.

Above. In this Provençal
farmhouse belonging to an
English family, interior
designers Anthony Collett
and Andrew Zarzycki opted
for the natural look. In the

children's bedroom,
the cladding is in painted
wood. Hazel wood has
been used for the bunk beds.
On the floor, there is a raffia
mat from Cogolin.

Above. This villa on the shores of lake Constance has been restored by Anthony Collett, John MacLeod and David Champion, who designed all the architectural features as well as the furniture. The attic bedroom is all softness and mellowness, with its white-painted, pine walls. A muslin veil has been draped around the corners of the iron four-poster bed, at the foot of which stand two Arts & Crafts stools. On the window seat and the armchair, ikats against a linen backdrop. The parquet floor is covered with a woolen carpet.

FOUR-POSTER BEDS & CANOPIES

WITH THEIR ROMANTIC HANGINGS AND DRAPES, FOUR-POSTER BEDS SEEM TO COME STRAIGHT OUT OF FAIRYTALES. DECORATOR ANOUSKA HEMPEL IS ONE OF THE GREAT CANOPY SPECIALISTS. IN HER HOTELS, SHE ARRANGES THESE BEDS IN A THOUSAND DIFFERENT WAYS.

Left. At Blakes Hotel in Amsterdam, we find the Anouska Hempel touch, with the interplay of ginger and charcoal gray stripes, in a bedroom the color of wonderful spices. On the walls, there is a collection of perfectly aligned mirrors. The window is covered with bamboo blinds.

Above. Anouska Hempel decorated the bedroom in a villa near Palma de Majorca in Spain. On the four-poster bed—framed by linen curtains acting as mosquito netting— she has placed a mass of straw cushions, in linen and cotton. Syrian stools are placed at the foot of the bed.

CANOPIES

Left. On Saint-Barthélemy in the West Indies, a Swedish woman fell head over heels in love with this superb colonial house, which she rescued from its neglected state. In her bedroom, there is a majestic four-poster bed beneath a diaphanous mosquito net. Delicate, Swiss cotton curtains filter the bright light from outside. Just a few pieces of wooden furniture and white hangings make up the decor. The result is a bedroom that is at once austere and feminine.

Right. Adeline Dieudonné, who runs the Noël linen company, has chosen to embellish this wood and straw bed with simple, white cotton linen that is embroidered with a verdure lattice pattern and enhanced by a mohair blanket. A small cushion, with salient-lined borders, matches the green motifs.

Left. For André and Françoise Lafon's home near Marrakech, in Morocco, Françoise handled the interior decoration. In her bedroom, around the traditional brass bed, she has arranged objects that were bargain-hunted in antique stores and found in flea markets.
Above. Still in Marrakech, in the property of Quito Fiero, interior decorator Jacqueline Foissac shrewdly mixes Art Deco and Oriental hues.

CANOPIES

Irène and Giorgio Silvagni,
celebrities in the fashion
and film world, fell in love
with a house in Provence.
As the months passed, they
turned their Provençal
farmhouse into an amazing
abode, by using colorful
and unconventional decoration.
For their daughter's bedroom,
they chose a Klein blue,
conjuring up Matisse. It was
Giorgio himself who created
the color by mixing the desired
pigments. He also made the
four-poster bed using recycled
materials (wooden planks,
furniture legs, etc.).
These clever and inventive
creations give the room
an unconventional and
fanciful charm.

100

ALCOVES

IN THE 17TH CENTURY, THE SPANISH WORD ALCOVE MEANT A "LITTLE BED-ROOM." THERE, LADIES OF POLITE SOCIETY, KNOWN AS "PRÉCIEUSES," WOULD RECEIVE THEIR GUESTS AND HOLD SALONS. THESE DAYS, BEDS NESTLING IN ALCOVES GIVE THE IMPRESSION OF COZY COMFORT.

Left. In this bedroom, with its Le Manach printed wallpaper, the headboard fits snugly into an alcove adorned with an 18th century architectural drawing. The mahogany bedside table was designed by Alain Raynaud.

The sheets and pillowcases are the work of Christian Benais. **Above.** In his 19th century apartment in Paris, Christian Benais has installed this decor—which was created for the 1991 launching of the Chanel perfume, Egoïste.

ALCOVES

A very neo-classical style was evident in Bill Blass' New York City apartment. The couturier chose neutral tones for the walls, which contrast with the mahogany parquet and the paisley pattern of the bed linen. In the middle of the room, the large mahogany pedestal table from the Empire period acts as a stand for an old reproduction of the Vendôme column. On the right, he had an equestrian bronze of Napoléon. This room exudes a very masculine taste, of neo-Palladian inspiration.

Above. Zurich hairdresser Rudolf Haene designed this bed for the guest room in his Swiss chalet. The bed was then made by a local craftsman.

The wood decor, combined with the whiteness of the linens and hangings, creates a pleasant feeling of comfort.

106

Above. In this bedroom of
Anglo-Indian inspiration—
where the bed is tucked into an
alcove—cupboards with small
shutter doors act as wardrobes.

A Bertoïa bench has been
placed at the foot of the bed—
which is covered with white,
antique linen sheets and a
printed silk bedspread.

ALCOVES

Top, left.
At Le Chaufourg, a Périgord guest house, this room is lit by two French windows and, above all, by this unusually large bull's-eye window. The rounded, wooden moldings are painted white and conceal large wardrobes. The bedside tables were specially designed and made by a local blacksmith. The cane bench is Napoléon III.

Top, right.
Still at Le Chaufourg, two family portraits hang on the ocher walls, which feature brushed and waxed rendered finish. The bed fits in an alcove where the dominant feature is a piece of Louis XVI woodwork. The floor has been created with different types of old terra cotta tiles.

Bottom, left.
The two oak sofas in the ante-room can be used as beds, if need be. They were designed by Anthony Collett and Andrew Zarzycki, as was the hazelwood bed. The carpet is a dhurrie purchased in London and cut to size.

Bottom, right.
On the Berber bed, an old, Provençal quilted bedspread and white linen. The walls are covered with tadlakt.

HEADBOARDS

MATERIALS, COLORS, PATTERNS: HEADBOARDS MAKE ALL MANNER OF WHIM AND FANCY POSSIBLE, AND CAN BE STRUCTURED LIKE ACTUAL SCREENS OR PARTITIONS. THEY CUNNINGLY ROUND OFF THE DECORATION OF A BEDROOM, AND LEND A TOUCH OF COMFORT AT THE SAME TIME.

Left. This headboard features vivid colors. The sheets and pillowcases are by Michelle Halard for Puymorin, and the yellow cushion comes from Porthault. The bedspread is by Portobello. The wooden surface comes from the Conran Shop, and the framed poster on the wall is from the Pompidou Center museum in Paris.

Above. In this room, the headboard, bedside table and bench table, all in ebony, were designed by architect Rémi Tessier. Muriel Grateau created the linen, and the reading lights were designed and made by Manufactor.

HEADBOARDS

Chic sobriety wins out in this
bedroom, where the screen
acting as a headboard can also
be used to hide storage units.
Made of fir wood, it is the kind
you can assemble yourself.

Left. A very relaxed kind of refinement is revealed in this bedroom, which juggles with the contrasts between dark wood and light paint. The ash wood shelves for objects and books were designed by Catherine Memmi, as were the linen sheets and Merino wool blanket. The curtains are made of silk lined with wool and angora.

Above. This headboard in Frédéric Méchiche's home is enlivened by the stripes he is so fond of. On the wall, a painting by Jean-Claude Blais is lit by a string of fairy lights. A 19th century plaster cast vase sits on the right.

Above. A 19th century Chinese screen brings an Oriental atmosphere to this house in Flanders, decorated by Lionel Jadot. A mixture of silk and velvet was used for the cushions, and velveteen for the studded headboard from Vanhamme. The four spiral bed posts are connected to one another by lengths of bamboo.

Right. A sober, clean design is present in this bedroom that plays with natural colors. Over the headboard, decorator Henri Becq has put a striking sculpture by Raphaël Scorbiac entitled *Twenty-one People Waiting for Happiness*. On each side of the sycamore bed—stained the color of rosewood—two stools in stained ash wood serve as bedside tables.

BATHROOMS

BATHROOMS, WHATEVER THEIR STYLE, HAVE BECOME FULLY-FLEDGED ROOMS IN THEIR OWN RIGHT. REFUGES. SAFE HAVENS. THE MOST PRIVATE OF PRIVATE ROOMS. IN THE 19TH CENTURY, DRESSING TABLES WERE PART OF THE BEDROOM. TODAY, MORE OFTEN THAN NOT, IT IS THE BEDROOM THAT ENCROACHES UPON THE BATHROOM—WITH SOFAS, PICTURES ON THE WALLS, WOOD PANELING, AND EVEN WALL HANGINGS. IN LARGE HOMES, IT IS COMMON FOR PEOPLE TO SACRIFICE A BEDROOM TO CREATE A LARGE BATHROOM. BUT FOR HOMEOWNERS WHO DO NOT HAVE ROOM TO SPARE, THE BATHTUB MAY END UP IN THEIR BEDROOM, WHERE THE MIRROR AND SINK BECOME PART OF THE DECORATION. THE TRULY ORIGINAL AMONG US TURN OUR BATHROOM INTO A SHOWPIECE OF OUR OFFBEAT TASTES. LOVERS OF THINGS CONTEMPORARY CAN HAVE A FIELD DAY WITH MINIMALISM, IN PURSUIT OF MATERIALS THAT ARE AT ONCE RAW AND REFINED.

BATHROOMS FOR LIVING IN

BATHROOMS CAN SERVE AS A WELCOMING PLACE WHERE THE PRACTICAL IS MADE PLEASURABLE. WHY NOT IMAGINE A BATHROOM FOR LIVING IN, WHERE YOU CAN ENJOY YOUR SOLITUDE, TAKE TIME TO RELAX IN COMFORTABLE ARMCHAIRS, AND MARVEL AT A MUCH-LOVED PAINTING.

Left. In Anthony Collett's London home, the walls are partly covered by painted paneling. The bathtub dates from the 1930s'. The floor is an oak and teak checkerboard. The Arts & Crafts armchairs have canvas-covered cushions. Each mirror hides a cabinet. The large painting is by David Champion.

Above. In this triplex in Lyon, designed by architect Rémi Tessier, the bathroom radiator is hidden behind a woven wooden blind. The floor is covered with sand-colored comblanchien (a type of limestone from eastern France). The walls are painted with marble powder, resembling matte stucco.

Left. In Ireland's Luttrellstown Castle, this bathroom, with its splendid dimensions, calls to mind certain scenes in *Barry Lyndon*. It is as sumptuous as it is comfortable, and reminds one more of a living room—with its two Chippendale wing chairs, its window seats, and chintz curtains. The lion's-paw bathtub, lit by a magnificent chandelier, holds court, so to speak, right smack in the middle of the room.

Above. Another bathroom boasts an amazing 19th century copper tub that has been restored and set in a bay-window adjoining one of the bedrooms. It exudes remarkable elegance for a bathroom.

Left. This immense bathroom, in France's Bagnols castle-hotel, in the Beaujolais region, is filled with rounded shapes. The upper half of the walls are painted in trompe-l'oeil, which serves to emphasize the shape of the bathtub, sinks and mirrors. And the wing chair gives the room the character of a living room.

Above left. The "Taller de Arquitectura," or "Architecture Workshop," in Barcelona, has been converted by Ricardo Bofill so as to combine warmth and friendliness with an atmosphere of contemplation. A low bath has been set into the floor of the bedroom. A triptych of pivoting mirror-shutters can be used to adjust the lighting in the room. The chair on the right is a reproduction of a Gaudi chair.

Above right. Silvio Rech and Chris Browne have decorated the Ngorongoro Crater Lodge, in Tanzania, in a Baroque style. Beyond the long silk curtains lies the savannah. The bathtub is covered in concrete and embellished by a piece of carved wood. Limed wooden paneling is affixed to the walls with large hammered nails. The Medici vase lends a touch of Italian style.

BATHROOMS FOR LIVING IN

In the home of the famous
Belgian couturier Edouard
Vermeulen, the bathroom has
been designed as a living room,
complete with pouffe and
armchair (Axel Vervoordt)
covered with white linen, and
Louis XVI cabriole chair.
An 18th century parquet has
been chosen for the floor.
The sink unit is in oak, with
the sinks set in black stone.

CONTEMPORARY
BATHROOMS

IN THE CONTEMPORARY BATHROOM, MODERN MATERIALS SUCH
AS SANDBLASTED GLASS, CHROME-PLATED NICKEL, AND RESIN ARE
COMBINED WITH SLATE, GRANITE, AND TRAVERTINE, TO FORM REFINED
LINES OFTEN COMPLYING WITH A CAREFULLY DESIGNED SYMMETRY. THE
HOMOGENEITY OF THE DESIGN IS INVARIABLY A CONSTANT FEATURE, AS
ARE THE BEAUTY OF THE ACCESSORIES AND THE CREATIVE USE OF LIGHT.

Left. In the home of decorator
and designer Agnès Comar,
the bathroom is lit by sunlight
from her private garden.
The sink and bathtub
are set on slabs of green slate.
The floor is pale oak parquet.
The towels are by the designer
herself, and the drawing is
by Suzanne Valladon.
Above. Decorator Jean
de Meulder chose natural
materials to cover the areas
around this bath in an
Antwerp townhouse. The room
is clad in dark green stone
from the Dolomites, as well as
white and green marble. The
bathtub is by Philippe Starck.
The room represents a
harmonious marriage of
minimalism and luxury.

CONTEMPORARY
BATHROOMS

This bathroom, in an old
converted farmhouse,
has been pared down to
a Japanesque-asceticism.
It is the result of
a stylistic exercise undertaken
by the architect Joseph
Dirand. The goal was to
create a bathroom that did
not show any technical
installations. On the wall,
a large mirror hides small
storage units and cabinets,
lights, switches, plugs, and
plumbing fittings.
The bathtub, floor and
sink unit are thick slabs
of Arudy stone, from the
Basque Country.

CONTEMPORARY BATHROOMS

Above. On the second floor of the "Starck House," the bathroom is all white, and basks in light filtered through Venetian blinds. At once spare and sophisticated, it includes an old-style bathtub, a unit with drawers, a bowl designed by Starck, and a large Venetian mirror from the Galerie San Marco. A Tom Dixon chair stands near the heated towel rack. The banister upright at the far end of the room has been extended by a pole to hold a lampshade.

Above. In Malaysia, the bungalows at the Le Dataï Hotel offer plenty of comfort on the edge of the jungle. The bathtub, fitted into an alcove, is flanked by two symmetrical sinks. The floor, tub sides, and sinks are all made of "balau," the local wood, while the surfaces of the sink units are in white marble from Langkawi, the island where the hotel is located. The keywords of the decoration here are exoticism and refinement.

Above left. Here, wood once again provides a contemporary ambience. In this home near Paris, decorated by Didier Gomez, cedar gives the bathroom its tone. There are inside shutters on the window, and two sinks are set into the stone top. Rods acting as towel racks are fitted to the front of the unit.

Above right. In the Amangani Hotel in Jackson, Wyoming, the bathroom floor is in sequoia wood. The room opens onto a private terrace. The various refined details include lemongrass soap, bath essences from Bali, and a black marble soap dish. The slatted wooden blinds serve to filter the light steaming in from outside.

Right. This summer bathroom in a house on the Ile de Ré, on France's Atlantic shore, was designed by A. Blanchet, and features double sinks set into an old workbench. Above the wood-clad bathtub, with its cask-like hoops, a teak-framed mirror hangs on the wall. The whole room is lit by small blue pendant lights from Italy.

CLASSIC BATHROOMS

REFINEMENT AND NATURAL MATERIALS ARE THE HALLMARKS OF A CLASSIC
BATHROOM. WITH NEITHER OVERPOWERING COLORS, NOR OUT-OF-PLACE
EFFECTS, THESE CLASSICS ARE ANSWERABLE TO NO FAD OR FASHION, AND
ARE AS APPRECIATED TODAY AS THEY HAVE BEEN THROUGHOUT THE AGES.

Left. Elegance and rigor define
this bathroom, decorated
by architect Eric Gizard.
The furnishings are covered
with mahogany veneer while
the rim of the bathtub and
the floor are of Indian slate.
In the back corner, a shower
is separated from the main
room by a clear glass door.

Above. In the Paris home of
Valérie Solvit, director of a
communications agency, the
twin 1940s' sinks and their
period faucets and fittings
are topped by antique ebony
frames turned into mirrors.
She has altered the bathtub
by replacing the lion's paws
with four large balls.

Left. This Holland Park home in London was decorated by Anthony Collett and Andrew Zarzycki. The bathroom is a celebration of light and beautiful materials. The tiling is marble, and the wooden blinds between the linen curtains filter incoming light. The low armless easy chairs, made by Adnet, are covered with a Canovas terry.

Above left. In the home of Monic Fisher, owner of the Blanc d'Ivoire company, the bathroom is completely covered with stoneware tiles. Above the bathtub, there is a shelf holding framed pictures and elephant statues. These decorative items show up well against the contrasting white background.

Above right. This early 20th century town house in Neuilly-sur-Seine, has been totally renovated by architects Daniel and Michel Bismut. The bathroom floor is in combe stone, while the walls and sides of the tub have been given a candle wax finish.

Above. At Luttrellstown Castle, near Dublin, Ireland, this very refined-looking bathroom, with its mahogany-sided bathtub and mahogany-framed mirrors, has the look of a living room— complete with chintz chairs and curtains, here reflected in the mirrors. The sink and accessories are in Victorian style, as are the copper faucets, which have been in this castle for ages.

Above. In Isabella Gnecchi-Ruscone's Paris apartment, decorated by Stéphanie Cauchoix, the paneling is carefully set off by the use of contrasting colors. The black and white panels, Napoleon III table with Scagliola top, and dark carpet with petit point, all strikingly embellish the room. The birdcage in front of the window provides a unique touch.

Above. In this Parisian apartment, antiques dealer and decorator Alain Demachy drew his inspiration from the Directoire style. The bathtub has molded wooden sides matching the storage cupboards. The pale shades of color surrounding it show off the old fireplace nicely.

Above. Art director of Marks & Spencer, Brian Godbold, has chosen every detail of the decoration in this cottage in Suffolk, England.

The bathtub is set into painted wooden cladding and flanked by two sinks. The carpet lends a cozy atmosphere to the place.

The armchair is covered with a Charles Hammond fabric. The round and intentionally small mirrors resemble portholes.

ECCENTRIC
BATHROOMS

THE BATHROOM REFLECTS THE PERSONALITY OF THE PERSON WHO CREATED IT. AS SUCH, IT ALSO OPENS THE DOOR TO EVERY FANTASY. UNIQUE ROOMS FEATURING DARING SHAPES AND MATERIALS, AN ENDLESS RANGE OF COLORS, AND STUNNING VIEWS FROM THE BATHTUB ARE ALL COMMON PLACES WHEN EXAMINING ECCENTRIC BATHROOM DESIGN.

Far left. In Provence, the daring style of Maxime de la Falaise crops up in this "patchwork bathroom," with its different Carocim cement tiles. Patch the dog takes center stage above the bathtub, which was found at a demolition site's, in—where else?—Bath! On the left, the "Marguerite" chair is upholstered African-style, so as to remain faithful to one of the sources of inspiration for the decoration of the house.

Left. This light and simple space blends well with the rest of Jacques Séguéla's home, which has been remodeled by architect Jean-François Bodin. In the middle of the bathroom, opposite the window, a Jacob Delafon bathtub, with its generous dimensions, sits imposingly. It has been refurbished and painted in imitation marble. The glazed wooden blinds are from Conran's in London.

Left. High-tech spirit and industrial aesthetics meet in this loft in Bruges, Belgium. The space was once an abandoned factory, but has been beautifully converted by architect Linda Arschoot. The jacuzzi tub has been raised to provide bathers with a view over the pool outside. The walls and floor are covered with faience tiles in two shades of green. The sinks and stainless steel faucets and fittings are by Starck.

Above. In Yves Saint Laurent's residence in Marrakech, the star-shaped bathroom mirror calls to mind the ponds in the Majorelle gardens. The walls are in orangy tadlakt, while the sides of the sink and tub are in green zelliges. Yves Saint Laurent entrusted the decoration and design of his house first to interior decorator Bill Willis, and then to Jacqueline Foissac. The wall lights are in 1930s' style.

Here is the bathroom of kings in the Ministry of Foreign Affairs in Paris. Two bathrooms were designed in 1938 by the Compagnie des Arts Français to mark the visit of the king and queen of England. The design was done in a very modern vein: spare lines, gold and silver mosaics, chrome-plated pipes, exploded glass.

Left. The king's bathtub features gilded tiles, faucets and handrails. The head of the bath contains a hidden light. Medallions of exploded glass are embedded in the ceiling frieze, and also serve to conceal lights. The floor is in sanded marble, inlaid with copper scallop-shaped designs.

Above. In the queen's bathroom, the pattern of the Labouré exploded glass wall-piece hides lighting. These creations, by the Compagnie des Arts Français, are reminders of the creative brilliance of artists of the day such as Adnet.

ECCENTRIC
BATHROOMS

Daring and tradition are the
hallmarks of Bettina Bachmann,
an American decorator based
near Oxford, England. In her
bathroom, the walls are painted
blotting-paper pink and apricot,
as are the walls visible through
the door to the right. The side
for the tub was designed by
Bettina and made by the local
blacksmith. The Victorian
chaise longue is covered with
heavy white cotton cloth, and
a jute carpet covers the floor.

COUNTRY BATHROOMS

TWO OF THE MOST PRIZED PRIVILEGES OF COUNTRY LIFE ARE SPACE AND NATURAL MATERIALS. PASTORAL COUNTRY SETTINGS INHERENTLY SPRING TO MIND THE VALUE OF REST AND RELAXATION. AND THE TRADITIONAL WIDE BATHTUB IS THE IDEAL PLACE FOR LETTING OFF STEAM, AND ENJOYING A MOMENT TO ONE'S SELF.

Left. Anna and Gunther Lambert decided to make a home of this old, 18th century manor house in Picardy. The upper walls of this bathroom are covered with a beautiful black Jouy fabric, while the lower part is made of lacquered white wood. The Gunther Lambert armchairs are in black rattan and wrought iron.

Above. One of the bathrooms in Yves and Michelle Halard's castle in the Berry region, France, has taken over a room it was not meant to be in, resulting in a bathroom with living room sensibilities. The walls are covered in a deep red Jouy fabric. The toilet table has been improvised from an old carving table.

153

COUNTRY BATHROOMS

Left. In Belgium, in the home of advertising executive and collector Marcel Cornille, the marble bathtub placed in the middle of the bathroom comes from a spa, and the faucets from Jermyn Street in London. Above the sinks, the two mirrors are framed in marble. A collector's spirit imbues this Flemish house with its simple, stout architecture.

Right. The attic area of this house on the shores of Lake Constance in Switzerland, has been used to create an amazing bathroom with a bleached pine sloping ceiling. The towel racks are set in a wooden frame that opens onto a cupboard. Anthony Collett and David Champion devised the decoration for the house by opening up the interior space, as much as possible, to the surrounding countryside. Here, two windows offer headlong views of the lake.

COUNTRY BATHROOMS

Inside the beautiful Mont-Blanc
Hotel in Megève, the pine
bathroom was designed
by Jean-Louis Sibuet—
who was responsible for
the renovation of the entire
building—and constructed
by a local carpenter.
The large bathtub has a sink
on either side, set in small
pine units. The result of
Sibuet's work is a room with
Nordic flavor in the middle of
Haute-Savoie, in the Alps.

Left. In Christian Tortu's home in Provence, the window that opens onto a garden courtyard is framed by two old-style kitchen sinks placed on simple wooden planks. An almost monastic, though contemporary atmosphere reigns here. The bathtub is set in a wooden casing.

Right above. This old house in the heart of Brussels features limed teak doors that were inspired by a colonial shutter, and brought back from Thailand. The early 1900s' sink and tub come from England, while the mirror, with its copper molding, was found in a café in southern France. The pair of park chairs of Belgian origin are in stripped fir. Surveying the bathtub is an English model schooner.

Right below. In the castle that they redesigned, at Châteaurenaud, France, Yves and Michelle Halard paid great attention to the bathroom. The parquet is limed in a gray shade which picks out the gray of the walls. The blue stripes of the curtains match the doors and the window. The prints are taken from Diderot's *Encyclopédie*. The bathtub and sink on legs are both antiques.

These three bathrooms are found in Bagnols castle, in the Beaujolais region of France.

Left. In this slightly attic-like space beneath the roofs of a turret, the two window alcoves house a pair of mirrors on old stands. In the middle, dividing the room into two, a bathtub is set in a generous wooden frame.

Right above. The bathtub here is set in a piece of wooden furniture, the upper part of which has been set off by a triple mirror, topped by a cornice.

Right below. A rustic, intimate atmosphere reigns in this bathroom, with its exposed beams and oak sink units. The antique marble bathtub has been set in the middle of the room, and the antique faucet juts from the mirror.

SINKS
AND SHOWERS

THE ESSENTIAL COMPONENTS OF A BATHROOM ARE SINKS AND SHOWERS.
WHERE THESE ESSENTIALS ARE PLACED VARIES ACCORDING TO THE DESIGNER'S
WHIM. WITH JUST THE SLIGHTEST BIT OF INGENUITY, A DULL BATHROOM CAN
BE TRANSFORMED INTO A COMPLETELY NEW ENVIRONMENT.

Left. The spare lines in the bathroom of this Parisian apartment perfectly represent the minimalist aesthetics espoused by its designer Christian Liaigre. A door made of exotic wood opens onto a sink hewn from a block of marble.

Above. For the Hempel Hotel in London, decorator Anouska Hempel designed this show-stopper of a sink in Perspex. The entire bathroom is lit by a powerful light embedded in the lower part of the sink.

163

Left. In the "Pierre Bergé" suite at the Lutétia Hotel in Paris, the marble bathroom was designed by interior decorator Jacques Grange. The room is highlighted by a sink on its iron stand and the marble paneling that runs around the floor.

Above left. Architect Axel Verhoustraeten decorated this bathroom using flambé blue stone and teak for the floor, and stone for the sink set in a counter top made of wenge. Fine metal mesh blinds hang in front of the small windows.

Above right. In her Chelsea apartment in London, interior decorator Kelly Hoppen has combined the natural with the elegant. A stone bowl is placed on a storage unit. Bathroom cabinets are hidden behind each mirror.

SINKS AND SHOWERS

Above left. A contemporary design was used for this porcelain sink, made to be placed on a piece of bathroom furniture or similar surface.

Above right. In the home of decorator Carole Fakiel, the bathroom walls are covered in ivory-colored industrial ceramic. Two kitchen sinks have been turned into sinks. The faucets are by Stella.

Left. This room in Kenzo's Paris home shows the refinement of a Japanese-style bathroom. The walls are clad with sycamore.

A very small, round sink in marble is set into a surface with a magnifying mirror to one side of it. The two facing mirrors hide the storage units. The small modular openings, and their triangle of canvas fabric, were created by Kenji Kawabata.

Below left. In the Devi Garh Hotel in India, this small marble bowl with a hole in it is to be used as a sink. It is set on a marble bracket.

Bottom left. Water pours into a stone bathtub by Boffi.

Below right. In the home of London antiques dealer Gordon Watson, the sink, with its antique-style faucets, is a nickel-plated metal bowl placed on a limestone counter.

Above left. In an apartment designed by David Champion and Anthony Collett, the shower is enclosed behind a simple glass door, thus creating an actual cubicle. The bath towels hanging on the heated rack are within easy reach.

Above right. For this triplex by the Bois de Boulogne in Paris, decorator Yves Taralon used the natural transparency of glass and the natural simplicity of wood. The bath side is in goyabon, a wood from Brazil, and the floor is in limestone.

Right. In the home of architect Aude Cardinale, in the sauna and spa area, a large iroko tub is set on the stoneware tiled floor. The tiles are hemmed by pebbles set in concrete.

169

Left. The double shower in this Antwerp home, is lit from the sides, giving the water a rather magical look as it gushes out of large shower heads. The walls are in flambé gray granite. The design is by interior decorator Jean de Meulder.

Right. In Luttrellstown Castle, in Ireland, this bathroom features a most unusual bathtub fitted with a jacuzzi and a shower. This type of sanitary installation was once used in monasteries. The concept originated from Victorian days.

KITCHENS

FRIENDLINESS INCARNATE, THE KITCHEN IS INCREASINGLY REPLACING THE DINING ROOM AND LIVING ROOM AS THE FAVORITE GATHERING PLACE IN MANY HOUSEHOLDS. NEEDLESS TO SAY, IT MUST BE FUNCTIONAL, FIRST AND FOREMOST, BUT ALSO WELCOMING AND ATTRACTIVE. FOR THIS, TODAY, ALL THE KNOW-HOW AND RESOURCES OF PROFESSIONAL INTERIOR DESIGNERS AND DECORATORS CAN BE CALLED UPON. WE ARE TAKING YOU INTO THE KITCHENS OF LUMINARIES LIKE CALVIN KLEIN AND DESIGN MAGNATE TERENCE CONRAN, BUT ALSO THOSE OF SIMPLER PEOPLE WHO HAVE MANAGED TO ARRANGE THIS "CROSSROADS" OF THE HEARTH AND HOME WITH TASTE AND IMAGINATION. YOU WILL FIND EVERY KIND OF STYLE HERE, FROM "COUNTRY" ATMOSPHERES COMBINING OLD MATERIALS, SECONDHAND OBJECTS, AND AN EYE ON COMFORT, TO MORE CONTEMPORARY—OR EVEN ECCENTRIC—KITCHENS THAT PLAY WITH MODERN DESIGN, FURNITURE WITH CLEAN, REFINED LINES, AND HIGH-TECH HOUSEHOLD APPLIANCES.

KITCHENS
DINING ROOMS

FRIENDLINESS INCARNATE, THE KITCHEN IS INCREASINGLY REPLACING THE DINING ROOM. IT HAS TO BE WELCOMING, BUT FUNCTIONAL AT THE SAME TIME. TO MEET THESE EXPECTATIONS, INGENIOUSLY, THE KNOW-HOW AND TALENTS OF INTERIOR DECORATORS AND DESIGNERS ARE CALLED UPON.

Left. In a triplex in Lyon, architect Rémi Tessier played with the lighting by creating a light shaft that serves as the principal light source for the whole kitchen. He paid close attention to the materials and their color—the furnishings are made of wenge and woven wood and the central table is slate.

Above. In his home near New York City, Calvin Klein elected to respect traditional New England style. The old floor is made of large planks of blackened pine, resembling ebony.

KITCHENS
DINING ROOMS

A new stylistic direction for
English interior decorators
Anthony Collett and David
Champion is evident in this
large and erstwhile Victorian
apartment in the heart of
London. At once welcoming
and refined, the kitchen has
fitted oak cupboards, which
they designed. The cornice,
decorated with an array of
celadon platters interspersed
with sheaves of wheat concealing
loudspeakers, is a salient
feature of this room. In the
foreground, a very handsome
arts & crafts table with
matching chairs conjures up the
spirit of a country kitchen.

176

Left. In this home, designed by Philippe Starck, the kitchen is part and parcel of the life of the living room. The well-lit working surface is flanked on each side by shelves of dark-stained wood and white lacquered cupboards with simple chromium-plated handles. The chandelier is in Venetian glass.

Above. Donna Karan's Long Island kitchen is functional and inviting, and often serves as a dining room for quick lunches. The central island, used for preparing food, is transformed into a dining table in such occasions. The white color and the view of nature conspire to create a sense of serenity.

Left and right. Valérie Solvit and her husband Antoine have always dreamed of owning a home in the heart of Paris. Their wish has come true in this duplex apartment, designed with the help of their antique-dealer friend, Christian Sapet. The rooms on the lower floor are the living room, the children's bedrooms, the library, and the kitchen. For Valérie, "luxury is mixing things." So she contrasted

beiges, taupe, and blacks, to
which she added touches of red
and green. Black predominates
in the kitchen and its dining
room area, lit by many lamps.
The ambience created is
intentionally convivial, so
that the kitchen would become
the area where meals were
eaten. The walls are painted
matte black and the working
surface is made of crazed lava.
The kitchen and dining room
floors are wooden parquet.

When Andrew Zarzycki and
his wife, Jill, set out to redesign
their London home in the heart
of Chelsea, they were keen to
apply a contemporary spirit to
classical architectural principles:
axes, symmetry, and proportions.
Andrew readily admits that he is
inspired by Jean-Michel Frank,
Adolf Loos, Joseph Pleznick,
and Hans Van Der Laan.
He designed the maplewood
kitchen furnishings which
were then made by John Spencer
Joinery. The black stone working
surface comes from Pietra San
Marco. Conceived by the master
of the house, the stove and
extractor hood were designed
by Gaggenau. Zulu baskets
made of braided telephone wire
embellish the heavy oak table,
made by Matthew Collins—a
craftsman who is invariably
entrusted with the furniture that
Andrew designs. The black
leather chairs are by Mario
Bellini.

KITCHENS
DINING ROOMS

Left. This kitchen using beige and white hues, was designed by decorators Anthony Collett and David Champion. It features cabinets in waxed maple, and the huge copper extractor hood, which soars over the hotplates, catches the eye immediately. The black granite working surface matches the grey slate floor, which is covered by sea-grass matting. The room is a proper dining room with its round, cloth-covered table and its upholstered chairs lending it refined look.

Right. Advertising executive Eric Poisson enlisted the services of decorators Jacques Grange and Christian Benais for the renovation of a castle built on the heights overlooking Nice in the early 20th century. They achieved a happy marriage between ancient and modern in this large kitchen dining room. The painted ceiling of the former study overlooks a genuine, professional range. The large copper family chandelier is a 19th century remake of a 17th century Dutch model. The wood and granite table was designed by Eric Poisson.

KITCHENS
DINING ROOMS

When the three giants of British
interior design—Anthony
Collett, David Champion, and
John MacLeod—arrived in
Switzerland on the shores of
Lake Constance to renovate
this castle, the first thing they
did was open up the interior
spaces to the natural light and
outstanding view. The kitchen
illustrates the success of this
idea. It is bathed in light and
overlooks a garden inspired by
Monet's at Giverny. Cherry wood
is used throughout, and the
working surfaces are in black
granite. A huge table—with its
oak top sanded and bleached—
stands in the middle of the
room. The blinds are electrically
controlled, and the nearby
beams serve as supports for
wrought iron lights designed
by Collett and Champion.

CONTEMPORARY
KITCHENS

FOR THOSE DRAWN TO CONTEMPORARY STYLE, THE KITCHEN OFFERS A CHANCE TO PLAY WITH MATERIALS, FURNITURE, AND HIGH-TECH APPLIANCES. AND EVERYONE CAN EXPRESS THEMSELVES ACCORDING TO THEIR NEEDS—WITH SPARE, SOPHISTICATED, AND ALWAYS FUNCTIONAL LINES.

Left. Interior designer Christian Liaigre's kitchen—on the Ile de Ré, on France's Atlantic coast—combines simplicity and elegance. The large, working surface made of oiled teak, with its blackened doors, accommodates a Czech & Speake sink and stainless steel hotplates. Teak shelving is used for storing utensils and dishes.

Above. In this kitchen, organized around a central island, the cherry wood doors were designed by Pepe Tanzi for Boffi. The ovens and the grill are by Gaggenau, the extractor hood in stainless steel and glass is by Atag, and the refrigerator is by General Electric. The floor is covered with natural flagstones.

CONTEMPORARY KITCHENS

In this Corsican home,
where the interior space
opens generously onto the world
outside, large windows survey
the majestic seascape.
As a result, the kitchen
dining room, and living room
are all awash in light.
The idea for the stainless
steel cupboard doors came
from a bar at Fizaris airport.
The working surface is made
of Corsican granite.

Left. Interior decorator François Catroux makes his home in a Parisian apartment, where he has managed to create an extremely austere but warm ambience. In keeping with the other rooms, the kitchen is done in white, beige and brown tones which help to set off the Persian blinds on all the windows. This room, which doubles as a dining room, is in oak. A generous wine rack is suspended in the wall above the table.

Above. Interior decorator Marc Held's kitchen, in Paris, reflects his fondness for detail. The kitchen unit, configured like a bar, is covered with marine plywood, and one side can be folded down to make more room. A delightful atmosphere emanates from this nook beneath the sloping roof, where every effort has been made to use the space without taking away from the comfort of the room.

Above. Suspended between sky and water, magnate of English design Terence Conran makes his home in the upper reaches of a building surveying the Thames in London. The kitchen has been designed as a professional space—marble work counter in the center, chopping block—and a strong sense of real kitchen and pantry. The stools and long oak table, doubling as a sideboard, were originally designed for a restaurant. Light plays a major role in this room, located on the same floor as the dining room and living room. Light pours through the glass roof and long windows, sculpting the volume by highlighting the wooden banister and rough concrete columns.

Above. In the heart of a village on the Vendée coast, perfume creator Annick Goutal and her husband have made their dream come true. The couple has created a home where they can enjoy quiet hours of work and relaxation, and leave all that Parisian stress far behind them. The result of their hard work is a well-lit and welcoming home, where the decoration has evolved in tune with favorite whims and wishes. All the rooms are arranged around a sunny courtyard, into which the kitchen opens. As in the case with every room on the ground floor, the kitchen is painted white.

Left. Designed by Rémi
Tessier in Lyon, this kitchen
is in pale and dark sycamore
with a Cenia stone worktop.
The kitchen connects with
the other rooms like in
a loft, which means that the
light circulates throughout.
Above left. In Brussels,
Axel Verhoustraeten created
this kitchen entirely with fired
fiberboard and stainless steel.

The stainless steel table has
matching utensils and the
floor is in Cascaie marble.
Above right. Redesigned by
Agnès Comar, this Valais chalet
combines Swiss tradition and
modern comfort. The kitchen
furniture and floor are in
natural birch, while the
working surface is slate.
The extractor hood and oven
are by Gaggenau.

Above and right. Near the Ourcq canal in Paris, architect Hervé Vermesch has converted an old tannery into a superb home. He did so by respecting the building's industrial structure. The fluidity and voluminous effect of an industrial loft have thus been preserved. No room has been completely walled off, and pillars have been used to separate different areas of the home.

Above. The kitchen is fitted with a soap stone working surface and a cathedral glass extractor hood.

Large damask stone tiles are affixed to the walls.

Right. Here we have a view of the entrance to the kitchen. On the floor, the parquet has been painted in two shades of grey to give the illusion of a carpet. The bar is in the foreground.

Above. By removing the interior walls in a small 17th century building near the Bastille in Paris, interior decorator Nicole Lehmann has breathed new life back into this town house. As the kitchen well illustrates, one of her priorities was to bring light into every room, regardless of its connection to natural light sources. One way of doing this was to create floors made of glass tiles. Following the 1930s' style chosen throughout the house, the kitchen has a very striking personality. It was made by the Serre Company, using carefully designed colors and materials. The chairs are by Mallet-Stevens. The frieze of irregular tiles on the floor echoes the room's basic hues: green for the glass, grey for the stainless steel, and beige for the stone-like rendering.

Above. In southernmost Corsica, an American fell in love with a plot of land overlooking the sea at Sperone. He then entrusted Guy Breton with the task of creating a Californian house on the property. The owner wanted to be able to gaze at the sea from every room, including the kitchen.

The decoration here combines wood and aluminum in most unexpected ways. Aluminum bistro doors seal off the storage cupboards.

Around the pine table, a set of American chairs —the "Institutional Chair"— in light aluminum, derive from The Conran Shop. Porthole lights add an original touch to the decoration.

CONTEMPORARY KITCHENS

Left. In their home in Paris, Bernard Roux and his wife have seen to even the smallest details. The area earmarked for the kitchen includes a central unit covered with Polyrey celadon green laminate, which divides the room into two. The working surface is covered with wenge to create a sense of harmony with the floor. On the left it houses a large stainless steel sink. On the right, tall stools have been brought over from the United States.

Right. Dominique Babigeon's task was to redesign a 19th century town house in Nancy. In doing so, she organized this kitchen so that it became a huge room for living in and replacing the dining room, as the owners requested. Light pours into what was previously a terrace, and the decorations used are quite sober: the kitchen units are in exotic wood, as is the working surface. The floor is oiled oak parquet. The stove and the extractor hood are by Atag. An original idea here is the galvanized steel unit placed to the left of the stove and used for storing kitchen utensils.

COUNTRY KITCHENS

WHEN FUNCTIONAL IS NO LONGER DE RIGUEUR, KITCHENS ARE GETTING BACK THEIR FORMER WARMTH AND COZINESS. THEY CALL TO MIND HOW MUCH WE LOVED THOSE LARGE LIVING ROOMS WITH THEIR LOVELY AROMA OF WAX, AND THE SMELL OF LOGS CRACKLING IN THE HEARTH.

Left. In the Ile-de-France mill where the Fourets live, the kitchen was designed with the help of interior decorator Alain Raynaud. The cupboards are made of sheet metal painted black. The floor is covered with recycled tiles, and the working surface is done in blue and white tiling.

Above. In this Périgord house, a stove has been fitted into an alcove and painted matte black, thus giving the impression of an old-style oven. Above it, a thick slab of slate, cut to size and polished, houses a hotplate.

Above. In the home of Parisian decorator Frédéric Méchiche, the functional character of the kitchen does not get in the way of the old-style atmosphere. All the furnishings are in 19th century pine. The warmth of the wood, and the 18th century terra cotta floor, contrasts with the black walls and the grey of the zinc and marble.

Right. This Bulthaup kitchen combines modern materials like beech wood, cracked tiling, and steel, with the charm of old objects. The room is extended by a veranda that adds both light and space.

Architect Axel Verhoustraeten
designed this warm and
serviceable kitchen for a house
located in a residential
neighborhood in Brussels.
He opted for slightly greyish,
pale sycamore for the
furnishings. Ceramic platters
rest atop the Classique table,
designed by Verhoustraeten.
As in the other rooms, we find
furniture by Christian Liaigre—
here, stall chairs in sycamore
with seats covered in cotton.
The working surface is made
of oiled blue stone.

Above. In this Provençal farmhouse decorated by Estelle Garcin, the owners have opted for a simple but refined style. Rustic chairs surround a farmhouse table beneath metal lamps. The cast-iron stove is made by Ambassade Renaissance.

Right. In his house in Normandy, actor Pierre Arditi has designed a kitchen where references to the past go hand-in-hand with modern technology. In this former cellar, the floor has been redone in stone and cabochons. Above the working surface is beautiful 18th century tiling from the Farnèse gallery. A Directoire table has center stage. Above the range hood and the oven is a 17th century still life piece depicting a game bag. This central work is surrounded by oil paintings by Pierre's father, Georges Arditi.

Left. Not far from Paris, architect Christian Duval and his wife have converted an old farmhouse into a lovely home. The varnished fir kitchen is the house's gathering place: the hanging baskets give it a homey feeling and the large windows open onto a small courtyard garden perfect for summer days. In the center, a preparation counter with a built-in sink and storage cupboards.

Above. This London kitchen was designed by interior decorator Anthony Collett and made by John Spencer. It is done in oak, and the working surface is in black marble. The floor consists of waxed elm planking. The central table is in oak, and was designed by Anthony Collett. The early 20th century lamp on the far table, and the chair in the foreground, come from Paul Reeves in London. The cast-iron stove on the left is a La Cornue.

Above. In this large residence in Genoa, the walls of the high-ceilinged kitchen are covered with prints, family photos, paintings, and drawings. This kitchen-*cum*-gallery is as functional as it is hospitable. A range hood extracts unpleasant smells, the appliances are all ultra-modern, and the waxed parquet adds to the warm effect of this friendly kitchen.

Right. The spirit of Provence holds sway in this very ancient farmhouse in the Alpilles, north of the Camargue. It has been renovated after spending four decades unhabited. The home's foundations date back to the 13th century, which explains the vaults in the oldest part of the house, where the kitchen is. Here, the table is laid facing the large stone fireplace, creating a scene from bygone days.

Above. In the old hunting lodge he lives in on the outskirts of Brussels, couturier Edouard Vermeulen has managed to combine modern design and traditional materials. All the furnishings and household appliances have been covered with broad planks of aged oak. A workshop table stands boldly in the middle of the room. The working surface is in black stone and the chrome-plated nickel taps are by Clek.

Above. In her Paris home, florist Dani decided to install an American-style kitchen bar. The walls of her studio are made of recycled planks. Behind the bar, covered with a sheet of zinc, are the sink, appliances, hotplates, and oven. The cupboard doors are old shutters. And, while this American-style kitchen concept may be very modern, the atmosphere created in the room is quite rustic at the same time.

Above. Here, with every house she lives in, Loulou de la Falaise projects her personality, her joy in life and exuberance into the decoration and interior design. This kitchen in her home in Normandy is covered with two-colored tiles.

Right. In this kitchen, tiling on the units and furniture is continued on the walls, and the cupboard doors have been limed in the same color as the tiles.
The working surface is in enameled lava.

ECCENTRIC
KITCHENS

THE KITCHEN MAY OFTEN BE THE HEART OF THE HOME, BUT IT CAN ALSO BE WHERE ECCENTRICITY IS LET LOOSE. IT MAY ACCOMMODATE THE MOST EXTRAORDINARY CHANDELIERS, OR RECYCLED FURNITURE ALTERED TO SUIT INDIVIDUAL WHIMS. COLORS EXPLODE AND DESIGN HAS FREE REIN.

Left. For a Parisian duplex, decorator Frédéric Méchiche came up with this functional kitchen. The floor is a checkerboard of old marble mosaics. The ceiling has been painted black and the cornice white, so as to match the black and white stripes hand-painted on the end wall. The working surface is in steel, and the furnishings in wild cherry wood.
Above. In this functional kitchen and dining nook, the kitchen units are in matte beige Formica, while the working surface and buffet are in mottled granite. In the foreground, the sofa is covered with black linen, and the stools are in steel and leather.

ECCENTRIC KITCHENS

Left. This all stainless steel kitchen was built by Bulthaup in an industrial loft in Bruges, Belgium, that was redesigned by architect Linda Arschoot and her husband Sweet Love. The space is completely open to the outside, and the original structure of this abandoned factory has been preserved. Small metal beams, cupboard doors, and porthole lights are done in the same metal. The floor of the mezzanine, which partly accommodates the kitchen, is made of yellow stoneware.

Right. In the Milan home of decorator Vanna Bellazzi, the kitchen is the pre-eminent room for living in. The walls are covered with plates, dishes, small mirrors, and other unique items picked up on bargain hunts. The 19th century table comes from a printing works. The Viennese chairs date from the Secession (Montessi and Garau in Milan). The striking chandelier is a combination of iron and pendant stones.

In a classic farmhouse in the Alpilles, just north of Arles, Maxime de La Falaise has created a Baroque home for her friend Sarah Saint-George. The daring and eye-catching design suits Saint-George perfectly.

Right. Above the green Aga stove, the Godin hood has swapped its copper for the simplicity of stainless steel. In the foreground, a long butcher's block that was unearthed in the Béarn, in the western Pyrenees, reveals a secret drawer. On the left, a cupboard painted by Maxime and an Andy Warhol canvas.

Above. The wicker drawers in this Aga stove unit hold cutlery and table linen. The marble sink and the taps are quite old. The mosaic is a mixture of gravel, pebbles, and bits of Venetian glass.

Above. The kitchen of architects Jean-Louis and Mado Mellerio is the only brightly colored room in their apartment. The atmosphere is convivial, with a central stove and island, which also serves as a table for informal meals with friends. The room was made by Bulthaup and the kitchen appliances are by Gaggenau.

Right. When adman Bruno Le Moult asked Philippe Starck to design his home in the Ile Saint-Germain in Paris, the result was an impressive space of concrete, glass, marble, and aluminum, for light to play off of. The kitchen is spectacular. The sink, in a block of marble, matches a floor covered in the same material. Against the far wall, there is room for a stainless steel worktop, a hotplate, and cupboards in sandblasted glass.

PATIOS AND VERANDAS

THE MAIN FUNCTION OF PATIOS, COVERED COURTYARDS AND VERANDAS, IS TO EXTEND THE INSIDE OF THE HOUSE TO THE OUTDOORS, OR TO BRING NATURE INTO THE HOUSE ITSELF. IN THE PAST, ONLY THOSE WHO LIVED IN WARM CLIMATES COULD EXPERIENCE THE LUXURY OF PATIOS; NOW THEY ARE FOUND EVERYWHERE. TO DESIGN BEAUTIFUL PATIO SETTINGS, LANDSCAPISTS AND DECORATORS UTILIZE ALL THEIR INGENUITY IN ORDER TO CREATE MINIATURE GARDENS OFTEN ACCOMPANIED BY TEAK FURNITURE, TERRA COTTA POTS AND PLANTERS TEEMING WITH FLOWERS AND OTHER AROMATIC PLANTS. OUT IN THE COUNTRYSIDE, COVERED COURTYARDS TRANSFORM OUTDOOR PATIOS INTO DINING ROOMS AND SUMMERTIME LIVING ROOMS. GREENHOUSES BECOME MULTI-PURPOSE ROOMS UNTO THEMSELVES.

TERRACES

IN LANDS WHERE THE SUN IS KING, SOUND PLANNING FOR THE USE OF VERDANT AREAS IS A NECESSITY. NO MATTER WHAT THE SEASON, A TERRACE—WHETHER IN THE COUNTRYSIDE OR IN THE CITY—PROVIDES A MARVELOUS PLACE TO GARDEN, RELAX OR RECEIVE GUESTS.

Left. This terrace floor features a far wall and furniture made of teak. Bamboo and ivy grow in flower boxes behind the wall. On the left, columns of ivy surround the bench. Box hedges, cypress, palm and olive trees grow in large flowerpots. The umbrella is Chinese.

Above. Landscapist Pierre Alexandre Risser has surrounded this teak bench with trimmed hedges, rose bushes and imitation jasmine. On the left is a magnolia tree pruned in the shape of a pyramid. In the foreground, Butterfly lavender and rosemary.

231

TERRACES

Left. Architect Laurent Bourgois has completely transformed this lovely, rectangular terrace in the heart of Paris. To give it more intimacy, he has covered the metal fence with a double trellis, and in the middle has placed earthen pots full of plants.

Right. Since the terrace connects the living room to the bedroom, a portico of iroko wood was installed to separate the two sections in a graceful manner. Jasmine and wisteria cover the portico which transforms the space into two distinct rooms of greenery. Plants and shrubs overflow from earthenware tubs decorated in iroko shingles. The flooring is made of stone slabs from Bourgogne.

TERRACES

Left. At Jacqueline Hagnauer's house, French windows from the living room open out onto the terrace, and help to extend those long summer days. Jacqueline has used a red and white color scheme. The red comes from her rhododendrons and climbing roses, the white, from anthemis, arum lilies and iberis. Since many of the plants—such as the box hedges, camellias and thujas—keep their leaves year 'round, she is surrounded by vegetation all year long.

Right. Laurence and Philippe Brunon's terrace is so large that landscapist Olivier Riols has planted a small herb garden on it. Parsley, chives, chervil and mint are separated at regular intervals by small hedges. The slatted floor is made of teak, and the chairs are draped in raw linen slipcovers.

Below. In Paris, an outstanding gardener has transformed her rooftop into a vegetable garden, mixing bulbs with roses, hydrangeas, strawberries, fennel, angelica and other aromatic herbs.

Right. In Milan, one dines on this charming terrace amidst the blooming roses and fruit trees—all of which lend a romantic air to the city.

TERRACES

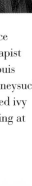

Above. On this terrace redesigned by landscapist Laurent Bourgois, Louis Benech has mixed honeysuckle, jasmine and variegated ivy along the lattice fencing at the edge of the balcony. Pittosporum and viburnum reside in the flowerpots throughout.

Right. The rear of the late Gianni Versace's house opens onto a garden patio enclosed by trellises and enlivened by a bubbling fountain. The result is an oasis of vegetation in the middle of Manhattan.

Left. Decorator Anne-Marie de Ganay had two stone benches made for the terrace of this country dwelling. Once a convent, it is now a private home. In the summertime, she places white cushions on the benches. In the evening, one can have a drink, watching the sun set on the Petit Luberon mountain range.

Below. Michelle Joubert has worked wonders with this château in Gignac. It was never finished, and had not been lived in since the 18th century. Terraces and ponds liven up the exterior of this family dwelling in the Vaucluse region. From one of the terraces, we have this view of the Luberon Mountains.

Left. All that was needed to transform this excessively long and narrow balcony were some meticulously chosen decorations and a carefully selected mixture of colored plants. This passageway has now become a cozy area where one can rest and meditate undisturbed, far from the gaze of others.

Below. This balcony has been turned into a beautiful terrace as a result of the careful management of every square inch of its surface.

A white tarpaulin has been attached to an arbor constructed to create shade. A cluster of clematis armandii and climbing Iceberg roses grow along the railing. In the planters, laurel trees, hellebores and box hedges.

Above. Kevin Baker has converted the rooftop of this small, three-story building in Seattle into a terrace. Although the maple trees aren't in bloom yet, large earthen pots filled with flowering white cyclamens remind us that spring is near.

Above. In the backyard of an apartment on the Upper East Side in New York City, we come upon this verdant patio. Two bamboo "curtains" define the space and seem to draw us into the summer dining room. The pair of forged iron lanterns are Moroccan.

Above. Meals are served on one of two terraces, depending on the host's mood. The "Malcontenta" chairs that encircle the stone pedestal table are originals. They were designed by English decorator John Stefanidis, and are based on a neoclassic design.

Above. This comfortable, white-walled, subdivided terrace is full of nooks and crannies. Here, "everything is done in order to make even the most difficult guest feel immediately comfortable, as if they were in their own home," says Millington-Drake.

TERRACES

Below. Tony Facella's Moorish-style home is situated between the sea and the medina of Hammamet. Its vast garden is arranged in layers of terraces that partially disappear amidst the vegetation. The summertime living room is comfortably furnished with Tunisian-style, sculptured wooden sofas and armchairs.

Right. "When designing a room, I consider the number of people that it will be able to seat," says Valentino, the famous couturier. "Discomfort, along with pretentiousness, is the worst error in taste that one can commit when decorating." Valentino obviously applied this philosophy when designing this terrace.

TERRACES

Above. In Tangier, nothing is obvious. But marvels like this terrace built off a house in the Casbah await us at every turn.

Above. In the Rothschild's
home north of the island of
Corfu, the terrace, bordered
by a stone bench, offers a view
of the port of Kouloura.

GREENHOUSES AND PATIOS

WHETHER ANNEXED TO A HOUSE OR INSTALLED AT THE END OF THE GARDEN, GREENHOUSES AND PATIOS CAN BE TRANSFORMED INTO DINING ROOMS, LIVING ROOMS OR PEACEFUL HAVENS. ALL ONE NEEDS IS A LITTLE IMAGINATION.

Left. This slightly raised winter garden utilizes a corner of the house where the family likes to gather and have its meals.

Above. This greenhouse patio is bathed in light, yet sheltered from intemperate weather. It has become a full-time living room.

Left and above. In Dominique Kieffer's enclosed patio dining room, the outdoor table—which is usually covered with a variety of pots—is on occasion transformed into a festive dining room table. On the wrought iron bed in the background, there are a variety of pillows covered in fabrics from a collection by Kieffer. The floor is covered in sea grass.

GREENHOUSES AND PATIOS

New York City designer
Muriel Brandolini has
transformed the patio at her
home in the Hamptons into a
dining room winter garden.
The dim light filtering through
the straw venetian blinds,
the Tunisian rug, and the chairs
by Marc Newson all seem to
conspire to create a warm and
cozy atmosphere. She has added
a table by Jansen, an Egyptian-
style upholstered settee
and imitation-bamboo chairs.

Above. In Pierre Bergé's garden in Paris, we find this patio. It is an island of greenery, with its Proustian-like charm and seclusion. The tableware is set on a table by Poillerat. On the left, a console designed by Louis Cane. The wrought iron chairs date back to the 1950s.

Above. For his office patio, Bergé asked François-Josef Graf to design a structure that would allow him a splendid view of the garden.

When Paris awakens, six Australian parakeets launch into song, and the light from the small lamps softly fades.

VERANDAS AND COVERED COURTYARDS

NEITHER COMPLETELY OUTSIDE NOR INSIDE, A COVERED COURTYARD SHIELDS ONE FROM THE HEAT, THE RAIN AND THE WIND. IT EXTENDS THE LENGTH OF THE HOUSE, AND ALLOWS A VIEW OF THE GARDEN. THE VERANDA IS AN ADDED BONUS—AN EXTRA SPACE WHERE ONE CAN RE-LAX AND RECEIVE GUESTS IN THE MOST PLEASANT SURROUNDINGS.

Left. In Yves Saint Laurent's home in Marrakech, the colors used for the veranda harmonize with the fountain, which is bordered by bamboo, coconut trees and oleander.

Above. The sheltered courtyard at Pierre Bergé's house borders a garden redesigned by Pascal Cribier. The armchairs were bought at Alexandre Biaggi's antiques store.

VERANDAS AND COVERED COURTYARDS

Left. At the Tahitian home of architect Pierre Lacombe, a pavilion has been erected at the far end of the swimming pool. There, in the shade of a wooden-tiled roof, his friends and family can enjoy a drink. The outdoor furniture is Indonesian, Indian and Polynesian. The pool overflows its walls. It is lined with slabs of green stone that blend in perfectly with the environment.

Right. This swimming pool in Bangkok is at the center of four traditional-styled pavilions. The roofs are typical of those built in Chiang Mai. Near the sofas, an earthen jar from the 19th century overflows with orchids.

VERANDAS AND
COVERED COURTYARDS

Above. In this open-air living room of the Amanpuri Hotel on an island in the Indian Ocean, sunlight reflects off the wood and the palm trees. The use of space, the shade and the flowers add to the serenity of the setting, inviting us to lose ourselves in relaxation.

Above. The design used for the railings of this veranda in Corsica mirrors that often used for railings in the Bahamas and the French Caribbean.

The cushions adorning the rattan sofas are covered in white linen. The hammock comes from a trip to Brazil. Guy André, Guy Breton, Boguslaw Brzeczkowski and Jean-Marc Roques, four architects of the GEA (Groupement d'études architecturales), conceived this house.

Left. Beneath the roof of this house in Corfu, a veranda living room awaits its guests for those warm summer nights.
Above. To prolong the enchantment, breakfasts are served on this veranda teeming with jasmine and wisteria.

VERANDAS AND
COVERED COURTYARDS

Above. Not far from Marseilles, buried deep in the heart of a pine forest in Provence, we come upon the Pastré family's dwelling. When the Countess de Pastré lived here long ago, she used this covered courtyard, with its high vaulted ceilings, as her summer dining room.

Above. In the 17th century, the Count de Grivel wanted to share the beauty of his property on Mauritius island with as many people as possible.

Soirees, cocktail parties and private receptions were held beneath this covered courtyard summertime living room.

Left; above, bottom. On the islet of Moyo in Indonesia, this open-air bungalow dining room of the Amanwana hotel is situated right next to a nature preserve facing the sea. The sofas are arranged in a comfortable fashion. **Above, top.** This luxurious veranda facing the Java Sea—where tortoises, whales and dolphins commonly frolic—has been transformed into a guest bungalow.

271

VERANDAS AND COVERED COURTYARDS

Left. Philippe Starck's house is located in the middle of a clearing on a property near Paris. Birch trees and rhododendrons surround the house, which is made of wood and glass. One dines on a veranda simply lit by ceiling lights with white lampshades. The owner created the table and chairs.

Right. This veranda is overflowing with charm. A good old sofa was placed here for the occasion. It is surrounded by a rocking chair, and chairs found at a flea market. Add an Adirondack chair hanging from the ceiling, made of ash wood from a kayak, and the setting is picture perfect.

Above. In Tunisia, sturdy pillars supporting graceful archways create a luxurious veranda in the front of this house.

The owners are delighted by the effect that whitewashed walls have with the white rattan furniture.

Above. In Hammamet, the closed universe created by Violett and Jean Henson in the 1930s. The colonnades are made of whitewashed sandstone. Beneath the vaulted ceiling, belladonna lilies and banana saplings reside.

VERANDAS AND
COVERED COURTYARDS

Below. When the weather is pleasant at this country house near Paris, breakfast and dinner are served on the veranda. Garden baskets are hung from the rafters, while a chest in the background is buried in begonias.

Right. On this veranda, the stone benches are decorated with mattresses and seat cushions covered in raw linen.

The tables are made of iroko wood—which is less expensive than teak, yet endowed with the same properties. The lamps are Indian urns with metal shades.

VERANDAS AND COVERED COURTYARDS

Left. This one-story house in Corsica faces both the sea, and a grove of palm and olive trees. Easy chairs await the owners under the pergola covered with bougainvillea.

Right. During long summer days, this sheltered courtyard of a house in the Cévennes region of France is perfect for enjoying the view of the plains of Languedoc.

Resources

ABC CARPET & HOME
(CUSTOM DRAPERY, FURNITURE)
www.abchome.com
P: 212-473-3000

AGA
(STOVES)
www.aga-rayburn.com
P: 800-633-9200

ALESSI
(KITCHEN ACCESSORIES)
www.alessi.com
P: 877-253-7749

AMANA (MAYTAG)
(KITCHEN APPLIANCES)
www.amana.com
P: 800-843-0304

**AMERICAN STANDARD
& PORCHER**
(BATHROOM FIXTURES, FURNITURE)
www.us.amstd.com
P: 800-223-0068

AMTICO
(TILES)
www.amtico.com
P: 800-268-4260

ANN SACKS
(BATHROOM FURNITURE, FIXTURES,
LIGHTING)
www.annsacks.com
P: 800-278-8453

ARCLINEA KITCHEN COLLECTION
(KITCHEN DESIGN)
www.arclinea.it
P: 212-758-8370

ARTISTIC TILE
(STONE, GLASS, MOSAICS)
www.artistictile.com
P: 800-260-8646

B & B ITALIA
(CONTEMPORARY FURNITURE)
www.bebitalia.it
P: 800-872-1697

BAKER FURNITURE
(TRADITIONAL FURNITURE)
www.bakerfurnitue.com
P: 800-59-BAKER

BARLOW TYRIE
(TEAK GARDEN FURNITURE)
www.barlowtyrie.com
P: 800-451-7467

BARNEYS
(ACCESSORIES AND LINENS)
P: 888-8-BARNEY

BERGDORF GOODMAN
(ACCESSORIES)
P: 800-558-1855

BISAZZA
(GLASS MOSAICS TILES)
www.bisazzausa.com

BOFFI
(BATHROOM FURNITURE, PLUMBING)
www.boffi.com
P: 212-431-8282

BOSCH
(KITCHEN APPLIANCES)
www.boschappliances.com
P: 800-866-2022
(major appliances hotline)
P: 800-944-2904
(home appliances hotline)

BRIDGE KITCHENWARE
(KITCHEN ACCESSORIES)
www.bridgekitchenware.com
P: 212-688-4220

BRITISH KHAKI
(HANDCRAFTED FURNITURE)
www.britishkhaki.com
P: 212-343-2299

BROADWAY PANHANDLER
(KITCHEN ACCESSORIES)
www.broadwaypanhandler.com
P: 866-COOKWARE

BROAN
(KITCHEN APPLIANCES)
www.broan.com
P: 800-558-1711

BROWN JORDAN
(OUTDOORS ACCESSORIES)
www.brownjordanfurniture.com
P: 800-743-4252

BSH THERMADOR
(KITCHEN APPLIANCES)
www.thermador.com
P: 800-735-4328

BULTHAUP
(KITCHEN DESIGN)
www.bulthaup.com
P: 800-808-2923

CALVIN KLEIN
(ACCESSORIES, LINENS)
P: 800-294-7978
(store locations)
P: 800-256-7373
(order number)

CANAC
(KITCHEN CABINETRY)
www.canackitchens.com
P: 800-226-2248

CAPEL
(AREA RUGS)
www.capelrugs.com
P: 800-382-6574

CASSINA
(CONTEMPORARY DESIGN)

www.cassinausa.com
P: 800-770-3568

CENTURY
(TRADITIONAL FURNITURE,
UPHOLSTERY COLLECTIONS)
www.centuryfurniture.com
P: 800-852-5552

CHAMBERS
(LINENS, ACCESSORIES, FURNITURE)
P: 800-334-9790

CHARLES P. ROGERS
(BEDS)
www.charlesprogers.com
P: 800-561-0467

CHEF'S CATALOG
(KITCHEN ACCESSORIES)
www.chefscatalog.com
P: 800-884-CHEF

CHELSEA GARDEN CENTER
(PLANTS, POTTERY, FOUNTAINS,
FURNISHINGS)
www.chelseagardencenter.com
P: 877-846-0565

CHRISTIAN TORTU
(VASES, FLORAL DESIGN)
P: 888-955-7550

CHRISTY WEBBER LANDSCAPES
(DESIGN & CONSTRUCTION)
www.christywebber.com
P: 312-829-2926

COLOMBO
(BATH DESIGN)
www.orionhardware.com
P: 800-226-6627

THE CONRAN SHOP
(DESIGN FURNITURE, LIGHTING,
BATHWARE, TEXTILES)
www.conran.com
P: 866-755-9079

COOKING.COM
(KITCHEN ACCESSORIES)
www.cooking.com
P: 800-663-8810

COUNTRY FLOORS
(TILES)
www.countryfloors.com
P: 800-311-9995

CRATE & BARREL
(FURNITURE, LIGHTING, TEXTILES,
WINDOW TREATMENTS)
www.crateandbarrel.com
P: 800-967-6696

CUISINART
(KITCHEN ACCESSORIES)
www.cuisinart.com
P: 800-726-0190

CZECH AND SPEAKE
(PLUMBING)
www.czechspeake.com

DACOR
(KITCHEN APPLIANCES)
www.dacor.com
P: 800-793-0093

DELGRECO
(LUXURY OUTDOOR FURNITURE)
www.delgrecoandcompany.com
P: 212-688-5310 (NEW YORK)
P: 954-889-0990 (FLORIDA)

DELTA
(PLUMBING)
www.deltafaucet.com
P: 800-345-3358

DENNIS MILLER ASSOCIATES
(DESIGN CHAIRS, TABLES)
www.dennismiller.com
P: 212-684-0070

DONGHIA
(FURNITURE, TEXTILES, UPHOLSTERY,
WICKER AND RATTAN, TABLES)

www.donghia.com
P: 800-366-4442

DORNBRACHT
(BATHROOM FITTINGS, ACCESSORIES)
www.dornbracht.com
P: 800-774-1181

DOWNSVIEW
(KITCHEN CABINETRY)
www.downsviewkitchens.com
P: 905-677-9354

DUPONT
(TILING)
www.corian.com
P: 800-4-CORIAN

DURAVIT
(PLUMBING, TUBS,
PHILIPPE STARCK DESIGN)
www.duravit.com
P: 888-387-2848

DYNAMIC COOKING SYSTEMS
(KITCHEN APPLIANCES)
www.dcsappliances.com
P: 800-433-8466

ELKAY ELITE GOURMET SINKS
(PLUMBING)
www.elkay.com
P: 630-574-8484

EMAUX DE BRIARE
(TILING)
www.emauxdebriare.com
P: 516-931-6924

ENDLESS KNOT
(CLASSIC, CONTEMPORARY,
TIBETAN RUGS)
www.endlessknotrugs.com
P: 800-910-3000

ETHAN ALLEN
(HOME FURNISHINGS)
www.ethanallen.com
P: 888-EA-HELP1

FISHER & PAYKEL
(KITCHEN APPLIANCES)
www.fisherpaykel.com
P: 800-863-5394

FLOU
(BEDS, BED ACCESSORIES)
www.flou.com

FRETTE
(ACCESSORIES, LINENS)
www.frette.com
P: 800-35-FRETTE

GAGGENAU
(BUILT-IN APPLIANCES)
www.gaggenau.com/us
P: 800-828-9165

GARDENTILE
(LANDSCAPE ARCHITECTURE
DESIGN-BUILD FIRM)
www.gardentile.com
P: 206-285-8503

GENERAL ELECTRIC
(KITCHEN APPLIANCES)
www.ge.com
P: 800-626-2000

GINGER
(ACCESSORIES, LIGHTS, HARDWARE)
www.gingerco.com
P: 888-469-6511

GRANGE
(FURNITURE)
www.grange.fr
P: 800-GRANGE-1

GREAT INDOORS
(KITCHEN APPLIANCES)
www.thegreatindoors.com
P: 847-286-2500

GROHE
(BATHROOM FITTINGS)
www.groheamerica.com
P: 630-582-7711

GUMPS
(ACCESSORIES, FURNITURE)
www.gumps.com
P: 800-436-4311

HABIDECOR
(LUXURY RUGS)
www.habidecorusa.com
P: 800-588-8565

HANSGROHE
(SHOWER EXPERTS)
www.hansgrohe-usa.com
P: 800-719-1000
(toll-free literature)
P: 800-334-0455

HASTINGS TILE
(STONE, MOSAICS,
GLASS, PORCELAIN TILES)
www.hastingstilebath.com
P: 516-379-3500

HELTZER
(OUTDOOR METAL, STONE,
TEXTILE AND WOOD FURNITURE)
www.heltzer.com
P: 877-561-5612

HENREDON
(FURNITURE, UPHOLSTERY)
www.henredon.com
P: 800-444-3682

HENRY HALL
(OUTDOOR TEAK FURNISHINGS)
www.henryhalldesigns.com
P: 800-767-7738

HERMAN MILLER
(HOME OFFICE FURNISHINGS)
www.hermanmiller.com
P: 888-443-4357

HICKORY CHAIR
(CLASSIC FURNITURE)
www.hickorychair.com
P: 828-324-1801

IKEA
(ACCESSORIES, FURNITURE,
LIGHTING, RUGS)
www.ikea-usa.com

JACUZZI
(JACUZZI)
www.jacuzzi.com
P: 800-288-4022

JANUS ET CIE
(INTERNATIONAL OUTDOOR
FURNISHINGS AND DESIGN
CONSULTING)
www.janusetcie.com
P: 800-24-JANUS

KARASTAN
(LUXURY CARPETS AND RUGS)
www.karastan.com
P: 800-234-1120

KENMORE
(KITCHEN APPLIANCES)
www.kenmore.com
P: 888-KENMORE

KITCHENAID
(KITCHEN ACCESSORIES)
www.kitchenaid.com
P: 800-541-6390

KNOLL
(DESIGN CHAIRS, TABLES, LOUNGE)
www.knoll.com
P: 800-343-5665

KOHLER & KALLISTA
(PLUMBING, BATH DESIGN)
www.kohler.com
P: 800-4-KOHLER
www.kallista.com
P: 888-4-KALLISTA

KRUPS
(KITCHEN ACCESSORIES)
www.krups.com
P: 800-526-5377

KWC FAUCETS
(PLUMBING)
www.kwcfaucets.com
P: 800-KWCFCTS

LABRAZEL
(FURNISHINGS)
www.labrazel.com

LACANCHE
(STOVES)
www.lacancheusa.com
P: 800-570-CHEF

LA CORNUE
(STOVES)
www.purcellmurray.com
P: 800-892-4040

LAFCO
(CONTEMPORARY FURNITURE,
ACCESSORIES)
www.lafcony.com
P: 800-362-3677

**LAWRENCE DESIGN &
LANDSCAPING INC.**
(BRICK PATIOS AND WALKWAYS,
RAISED PATIOS AND PORCHES)
www.lawrencelandscaping.com
P: 716-289-4814

LEFROY BROOKS
(PERIOD-PIECE BATHROOM DESIGN,
PLUMBING)
www.lefroybrooks.com
P: 212-226-2242
(toll-free customer service)

LES MIGRATEURS
(FURNITURE, UPHOLSTERY)
www.lesmigrateurs.com
P: 207-846-1430

LINDA HORN
(ANTIQUES)
www.lindahorn.com
P: 800-772-8008

LLYOD FLANDERS
(ALL-WEATHER WICKER AND
ALUMINUM FURNITURE)
www.lloydflanders.com
P: 888-227-2852

M & M DESIGN INTERNATIONAL
(ORIENTAL AND
CUSTOM RUGS)
www.mandmgallery.com
P: 516-456-0681

MAINE COTTAGE
(WICKER FURNITURE)
www.mainecottage.com
P: 207-846-1430

MCGUIRE
(RATTAN, WOVEN AND TEAK
FURNITURE)
www.bakerfurniture.com
P: 800-662-4847

MCKINNON & HARRIS
(WROUGHT ALUMINUM GARDEN
SEATS, TABLES)
www.mckinnonharris.com
P: 804-358-2385

MECOX GARDENS
(ANTIQUE GARDEN ORNAMENTS)
www.mecoxgardens.com
P: 212-249-5301 (NEW YORK)
P: 561-805-8611 (FLORIDA)

MERILLAT
(CABINETRY)
www.merillat.com
P: 866-850-8557

**MICHAEL AZIZ
ORIENTAL RUGS**
(PAKISTAN RUGS)
www.michaelazizrugs.com
P: 212-686-8755

MICHAEL TAYLOR DESIGNS
(OUTDOOR FURNITURE)
www.michaeltaylordesigns.com

MIELE
(KITCHEN APPLIANCES)
www.mieleusa.com
P: 800-843-7231

MIROIRS BROT
(MIRRORS, ACCESSORIES)
www.frenchreflection.com
P: 800-421-4404

MODERNICA
(STAINLESS STEEL FURNITURE)
www.modernica.net
P: 323-934-1254

MOLTENI
(CONTEMPORARY FURNITURE)
www.molteni.it
P: 201-585-9420

MOEN
(BATH DESIGN)
www.moen.com
P: 800-BUY-MOEN

NOURISON
(HANDMADE RUGS)
www.nourison.com
P: 800-223-1110

ODEGARD
(LUXURY CARPETS)
www.odegardinc.com
P: 800-670-8836

OGGETTI
(ACCESSORIES)
www.oggetti.com
P: 305-576-1044

OLY
(HANDCRAFTED FURNITURE)
www.olystudio.com
P: 510-644-1870

OXO
(KITCHEN ACCESSORIES)
www.oxo.com
P: 800-545-4111

PARIS CERAMICS
(CERAMIC TILES)
www.parisceramics.com
P: 888-845-3487

PIER 1 IMPORTS
(ACCESSORIES, FURNITURE, WINDOW TREATMENTS)
www.pier1.com

PIERCE MARTIN
(OUTDOORS FURNISHINGS, ACCESSORIES)
www.piercemartin.com
P: 800-334-8701

PLAIN & FANCY
(KITCHEN CABINETRY)
www.plainfancycabinetry.com
P: 800-447-9006

POGGENPOHL
(KITCHEN DESIGN)
www.poggenpohl-usa.com
P: 800-987-0553

POLIFORM USA
(CONTEMPORARY FURNITURE)
www.poliformusa.com
P: 888-POLIFORM

PORTHAULT
(ACCESSORIES, LINENS)
www.dporthault.fr
P: 212-688-1660

POTTERY BRAN
(ACCESSORIES, FURNITURE, LAMPS, WINDOW COVERINGS)
www.potterybarn.com
P: 888-779-5176

PRATESI
(ACCESSORIES, LINENS)
www.pratesi.com
P: 800-332-6925

RALPH LAUREN
(BATHWARE, ACCESSORIES, TEXTILES)
www.rlhome.polo.com
P: 888-475-7674

RECYCLING THE PAST
(GARDEN STATUARY, PLANTERS, FOUNTAINS)
www.recyclingthepast.com
P: 609-660-9790

RENOVATOR'S SUPPLY
(KITCHEN ACCESSORIES)
www.rensup.com
P: 800-659-2211

REPERTOIRE
(CONTEMPORARY FURNITURE)
www.repertoire.com
P: 212-219-8159

RESTORATION HARDWARE
(ACCESSORIES, FURNITURE,)
www.restorationhardware.com
P: 800-762-1005

RICHARD SCHULTZ
(MODERN GARDEN FURNITURE)
www.richardschultz.com

ROBERN
(BATHROOM FURNITURE, ACCESSORIES)
www.robern.com
P: 800-877-2376

ROCHE BOBOIS
(PERIOD AND STYLE FURNITURE)
www.roche-bobois.com
P: 800-972-8375

RÖSLE
(KITCHEN ACCESSORIES)
www.rosleusa.com
P: 302-326-4801

RUTT
(KITCHEN DESIGN, CABINETRY)
www.rutt1.com
P: 800-220-7888

SCREEN TIGHT
(PORCH-ENCLOSING VINYL SLIDING SCREENS)
www.screentight.com
P: 800-768-7325

SEIBERT & RICE
(ITALIAN TERRA COTTA PLANTERS, URNS, ACCESSORIES)
www.seibert-rice.com
P: 973-467-8266

SIEMATIC
(KITCHEN DESIGN)
www.siematic.com
P: 800-959-0109

SMITH & HAWKEN
(PLANTS, FLOWERS, ACCESSORIES, GARDENING TOOLS)
www.smithandhawken.com
P: 800-940-1170

SNAIDERO
(KITCHEN DESIGN)
www.snaidero.com
P: 310-516-8499

STEAMASTER
(HOME SPA)
www.steamist.com
P: 201-933-5800

STELTON
(KITCHEN ACCESSORIES)
www.stelton.com
P: 651-690-0060

STOREHOUSE
(FURNITURE, UPHOLSTERY)
www.storehouse.com
P: 888-STOREHOUSE

SUB-ZERO/WOLF
(PLUMBING)
www.subzero.com
P: 800-222-7820

SUN BOSS CORPORATION
(PATIO CONSTRUCTION, AWNINGS, WALKWAYS, ELECTRICAL NEEDS)
www.sunboss.com
P: 909-782-2360

SUR LA TABLE
(KITCHEN ACCESSORIES)
www.surlatable.com
P: 800-243-0852 (ordering)
P: 866-328-5412
(customer service)

SUTHERLAND
(CLASSIC TEAK FURNITURE)
www.sutherlandteak.com
P: 800-717-8325

TARGET
(ACCESSORIES)
www.target.com
P: 800-440-0680

TOTO
(FITTINGS, ACCESSORIES)
www.totousa.com
P: 800-350-8686

TROPITONE
(PATIO FURNITURE, ACCESSORIES)
www.tropitone.com
P: 800-654-7000

U-LINE
(BUILT-IN APPLIANCES)
www.u-line.com
P: 414-354-0300

URBAN ARCHAEOLOGY
(FURNITURE, FIXTURES, ACCESSORIES, LIGHTING)
www.urbanarchaeology.com
P: 212-431-4646

VARENNA
(KITCHEN DESIGN)
www.varenna.com
P: 877-VARENNA

VENTAHOOD
(HOODS)
www.ventahood.com
P: 972-235-5201

VIKING
(BUILT-IN KITCHEN APPLIANCES)
www.vikingrange.com
P: 888-845-4641

WALKER ZANGER
(STONE, CERAMIC TILES)
www.walkerzanger.com
P: 877-611-0199

WAMSUTTA/SPRINGS
(ACCESSORIES, LINENS)
www.springs.com
P: 888-WAMSUTTA

WATERWORKS
(FURNITURE, FIXTURES, ACCESSORIES, LIGHTING, TILES)
www.waterworks.com
P: 800-998-BATH

WEST ELM
(ACCESSORIES, LINENS, HOME FURNISHINGS)
www.westelm.com
P: 866-428-6468

WICKER WORKS
(WICKER, RATTAN, IRON, TEAK, CARVED WOOD AND WOVEN HEMP FURNITURE)
www.thewickerworks.com
P: 415-970-5400

WHITE HOUSE
(LINENS)
www.the-white-house.com
P: 888-942-7528

WILLIAMS-SONOMA
(FURNITURE AND ACCESSORIES)
www.williams-sonoma.com
P: 877-812-6235

WM. OHS
(CABINETRY)
www.wmohs.com
P: 303-371-6550

WOODMODE
(CABINETRY)
www.wood-mode.com

WE WOULD LIKE TO THANK THE OWNERS, DECORATORS, INSTITUTIONS OR HOTELS THAT HAVE WELCOMED *ELLE DECOR* COLLABORATORS FOR THEIR STORIES:

PIERRE ARDITI, MAÏME ARNODIN, LINDA ARSCHOOT, DOMINIQUE BABIGEON, BETTINA BACHMANN, KEVIN BAKER, MEHMET BAY, HENRI BECQ, MICHÈLE AND PAUL BELAICHE, VANNA BELLAZZI, CHRISTIAN BENAIS, LOUIS BENECH, PIERRE BERGE. ALEXANDRE BIAGGI, DANIEL AND MICHEL BISMUT, A. BLANCHET, BILL BLASS, JEAN-FRANÇOIS BODIN, RICARDO BOFILL, LAURENT BOURGOIS, MURIEL BRANDOLINI, GUY BRETON, CHRIS BROWNE, LAURENCE AND PHILIPPE BRUNON, MANUEL CANOVAS, AUDE CARDINALE, FRANÇOIS CATROUX, STEPHANIE CAUCHOIX, DAVID CHAMPION, JEAN-ANDRE AND GENEVIEVE CHARIAL, ANTHONY COLLETT, AGNES COMAR, TERENCE CONRAN, MARCEL CORNILLE, PASCAL CRIBIER, DANI, ANNE-MARIE DE GANAY, TERRY AND JEAN DE GUNZBURG, LOULOU DE LA FALAISE, MAXIME DE LA FALAISE, JEAN DE MAULDER, ALAIN DEMACHY, ADELINE DIEUDONNE, JOSEPH DIRAND, CHRISTIAN DUVAL, TONY FACELLA, CAROLE FAKIEL, QUITO FIERO, MONIC FISCHER, JACQUELINE FOISSAC, B. AND O. FOURET, PATRICK AND YVELINE FRECHE, JEAN GALVANI, ZEYNEP GARAN, ESTELLE GARCIN, YVES GASTOU, ERIC GIZARD, ISABELLA GNECCHI-RUSCONE, BRIAN GODBOLD, DIDIER GOMEZ, ANNICK GOUTAL, FRANÇOIS-JOSEF GRAF, JACQUES GRANGE, RUDOLF HAENE, JACQUELINE HAGNAUER, YVES AND MICHELLE HALARD, MARC HELD, ANOUSKA HEMPEL, VIOLETT AND JEAN HENSON, KELLY HOPPEN, LIONEL JADOT, JOSEPH, MICHELLE JOUBERT, DONNA KARAN, KENZO, DOMINIQUE KIEFFER, DANIEL KIENER, CALVIN KLEIN, PIERRE LACOMBE, ANDRE AND FRANÇOISE LAFON, ANNA AND GÜNTHER LAMBERT, HUBERT LE GALL, JACQUES LEGUENNEC, NICOLE LEHMANN, BRUNO LE MOULT, CHRISTIAN LIAIGRE, JOHN MAC LEOD, FREDERIC MÉCHICHE, JEAN-LOUIS AND MADO MELLERIO, CATHERINE MEMMI, TEDDY MILLINGTON-DRAKE, JOËLLE MORTIER-VALLAT, WALDA PAIRON, ERIC POISSON, JULIE PRISCA, ALAIN RAYNAUD, SILVIO RECH, MICHELE REDELE, OLIVIER RIOLS, PIERRE ALEXANDRE RISSER, BERNARD ROUX, SARAH SAINT-GEORGE, YVES SAINT LAURENT, CHRISTIAN SAPET, JACQUES SEGUELA, BRIGITTE SEMTOB, IRENE AND GIORGIO SILVAGNI, VALERIE SOLVIT, ROGER SOUVEYRENS, JOHN SPENCER, PHILIPPE STARCK, YVES TARALON, REMI TESSIER, CHRISTIAN TORTU, VALENTINO, AXEL VERHOUSTRAETEN, HERVE VERMESCH, EDOUARD VERMEULEN, GIANNI VERSACE, AXEL VERVOORDT, GORDON WATSON, LADY WEINBERG, BILL WILLIS, ANDREW AND JILL ZARZYCKI.

PHOTOGRAPHS BY

Alexandre Bailhache: pp. 103, 154, cover bottom left. **Gilles Bensimon:** p. 175. **Guy Bouchet:** pp. 266, 267. **Gilles de Chabaneix:** pp. 41, 71, 84-85, 93, 135, 158, 166 bottom, 168 right, 180-181, 193, 194-195, 200, 205, 221, 226, 248, 264, 269, 274-275. **Philippe Costes:** pp. 166 top right, 167 bottom left. **Véra Cruz:** p. 88. **Jérôme Darblay:** pp. 214, 268. **Jacques Dirand:** pp. 18, 20-21, 34-35, 36-37, 38, 60, 68-69, 70, 78, 89,115, 125 left, 130-131, 132, 134 right, 145, 159 top, 167 right, 178, 179, 188, 190-191, 201, 202, 206, 220, 265, 272, 273, 279. **Rétro Güntli:** p. 106. **Marianne Haas:** pp. 10-11, 24, 32, 39, 54, 58, 64-65, 76-77, 79, 94-95, 98-99, 100-101, 102, 104-105, 109 bottom, 111, 121, 134 left, 141, 147-151, 164, 174, 185, 189, 192, 196, 197 right, 198-199, 204, 210, 213, 215, 217, 234, 242-243, 244, 246, 247, 249, 250-254, 256-257, 262, cover top right, cover center left, cover top left. **François Halard:** p. 218. **Eric d'Hérouville:** p. 125 right. **Séline Keller:** pp. 16-17, 117. **Daniel Kessler:** p. 152. **Vincent Knapp:** p. 128. **Guillaume de Laubier:** pp. 8-9, 12-13, 14, 15, 19, 22, 24-25, 26-27, 28-29, 30-31, 33, 40, 42-43, 44-45, 46-47, 48-49, 50-51, 52-53, 59, 61, 66-67, 74-75, 82-83, 86-87, 91, 92, 96, 107, 108, 109 top, 114, 116, 120, 122-123, 124, 126-127, 129, 133, 136-137, 138-139, 140, 142-143, 144, 146, 153, 155, 156-157, 159 bottom, 160-161, 162-163, 165, 166 top left, 168 left, 169-171, 176-177, 182-184, 186-187, 197 left, 207, 208-209, 211, 212, 216, 219, 222-225, 227, 232-233, 235, 237, 238-239, 241, 255, 258-259, 270, 271, 276-277, 278, 279, cover bottom right. **Didier Massard:** p. 110. **Nicolas Mathéus:** pp. 260-261, 263. **Patrice Pascal:** pp. 112-113. **Antoine Rozès:** p. 97. **Edouard Sicot:** pp. 56-57, 73, 90. **Patrick Smith:** p. 203. **Gilles Trillard:** pp. 55, 72, 230-231, 236. **Fritz Von Den Schulenburg/Inside:** pp. 80-81. **Deidi Von Schaewen:** p. 167 top left.

STORIES PRODUCED BY

Alexandra d'Arnoux: pp. 96, 102-103, 227, 262, 275. **François Baudot:** pp. 104-105, 125 left, 141, 175, 178, 180, 218, 239, 249. **Marie-Claire Blanckaert:** pp. 8-9, 11, 12-13, 14-15, 16-17, 18-19, 21, 23, 24-25, 28-29, 30-31, 32-33, 34-35, 36-37, 39, 40, 42-43, 44-45, 46-47, 48-49, 50-51, 52-53, 54-55, 56-57, 59, 60-61, 64-65, 66-67, 68-69, 70, 72-73, 74-75, 76-77, 79, 82-83, 86-87, 88-89, 90-91, 92, 94-95, 97, 98-99, 100-102, 106-107, 108-109, 111, 112-113, 114-117, 120-124, 126-131, 133, 134, 136-139, 140, 142-144, 146-153, 155-163, 164-165, 166 top left, 168-171, 174, 176-177, 180-184, 186-187, 189, 192-193, 196-197, 200-201, 203, 206-217, 219-225, 230-238, 240-245, 254-259, 264-271, 276-279, cover top right, cover center left, cover top left, cover bottom right. **Barbara Bourgois:** pp. 85, 110, 132, 135, 198-199, 272-273. **Michel Déon:** p. 93. **Geneviève Dortignac:** p. 38. **Laurence Dougier:** pp. 125 right, 260-261, 263. **Marie-Claude Dumoulin:** pp. 41, 71, 166 bottom, 195, 205, 226, 248, 272-273, 275. **Brigitte Forgeur:** p. 154. **Niccolo Grassi:** pp: 250-253. **Marie Kalt:** pp. 78, 167 right, 179, 194, 253, 274, cover bottom left. **Françoise Labro:** pp. 22, 26-27, 145, 185, 190-191, 202, 204, 265. **Gérard Pussey:** p. 58. **Catherine Scotto:** pp. 20, 166 top right, 167 bottom left. **Elsa Simon:** p. 188. **Paul-Marie Sorel:** p. 84. **Laure Verchère:** p. 10.

Translations

Living Rooms, Bedrooms, Bathrooms, Kitchens: Simon Pleasance and Fronza Woods
Patios and Verandas: Fern Malkine-Falvey

The Elle Decor Home is a compilation of the best stories previously published by
Filipacchi Publishing in the Portfolios series of books: *Kitchens, Bathrooms*
(published in 2002); *Living Rooms, Bedrooms, Patios and Verandas* (published in 2003).

Elle Decor (U.S.) and *Elle Décoration* (France) are both imprints of the Hachette
Filipacchi Media group. The content of these books was taken solely from
Elle Décoration and appeared only in France.